RETIREMENT PLANNING

SEVEN WAYS TO BE PREPARED

OA INC

CONTENTS

GIFT

Just For You!

A FREE GIFT TO OUR READERS

Tips for managing your personal finance that you can download and begin to implement right away! Scan QR code or visit link below:

http://oainc.activehosted.com/f/1

INTRODUCTION

"DO NOT SIMPLY RETIRE FROM SOMETHING, HAVE
SOMETHING TO RETIRE TO."

~ Harry Emerson

Living in the fear of never being able to pay off your debts is terrible. Given the current situation, money seems to be a problem for every single person. With rising inflation comes debt and more expenses that never seem to end. There are those out there who are in desperate need of financial planning and expert advice for how to handle their crisis and plan smartly for their retirement.

When all the expenses seem never-ending, and the burden of debt keeps you under pressure, you may be on the verge of stressing yourself out, as the feelings are overwhelming. You are just trying your best to find a ticket out of this dark scenario, and any ray of hope you see, you'll go for it. Trust us; we have been there, experienced it, and come out of it stronger and more knowledgeable than ever before.

If you are young, the idea of retiring early might seem impossible right now. Usually, young people are quite busy planning their careers or families or even settling down in new locations. Therefore, it is understandable that they may be reluctant to start thinking about retirement. Nevertheless, life goes on, and in times like these, quite fast. Every year, people postpone their plans regarding retirement. It ultimately means that they are moving further away year after year from securing an early retirement and having a good time in their golden years.

One of the most important priorities in your life should be to retire early with financial freedom and security. Though this is only worthwhile if it can be acquired through a financially comfortable and stress-free lifestyle. If you keep yourself under the pressure of overwhelming debt and living paycheck to paycheck, you won't be able to retire early. Unless, of course, you hit a jackpot and win the lottery!

People are stressed out, and that forces them to take out loans or live on low earnings. Individuals are losing their livelihoods, particularly since the pandemic and the dramatic shift in the global economy. Employment of any kind is in jeopardy, and people wake up every morning fearing that they may be dismissed that day.

Such stressful moments can push people into depression and, in rare circumstances, some become suicidal when their jobs are threatened and they have nowhere to go.

Nobody should be put through such ordeals, and we

believe there are always alternatives to overcome your difficulties and begin living a stress-free life. We understand that life can never be fully stress-free; otherwise, why would it be called living? When life throws you a curveball, do yourself a favor and throw it back at life by overcoming it.

There are numerous options for living a prosperous and debt-free life. When you have paid off all of your liabilities and all of your credit cards, the feeling is truly unforgettable! The happiness and fulfillment that comes from paying off one's debts is unmatched. You have complete control over how you spend your money. There are no limitations on how you spend your money. You get to buy things based on your preferences rather than their price tags. What might a person do with all of their money if there were no debts to pay? I'll leave that up to you to ponder.

All you need is someone to navigate you through the steps of financial planning and retirement. What if we told you that there are simple tips to steer clear of your debts while earning those extra dollars, worth building fortunes along the way? Sounds intriguing, right? And, are you really worried about where to invest, save, or earn your money efficiently? If that is the case, prepare yourself to learn seven great tips on how to regain control of your financial life, improve your life, and make your way towards that ideal retirement you always wanted.

Who Should Read This Book?

This book is going to do wonders for particularly the millennials and the debtors. More probably, the individuals seeking ways to keep earning even after they have retired from their long-term jobs. It is strongly recommended to those who are looking for a way out of their debts and who want to build wealth along their journey through life.

This book is for people looking to plan for their early retirement. It will take you through the retirement planning process and will provide useful ideas for opportunities after retirement as well.

Why Us?

Wondering why you should trust someone's advice is natural.

"Why am I supposed to listen to this narrator trying to dictate my financial life?" Well, for one, we are not dictators–we have been there ourselves and have experienced exactly what you might be experiencing, and that makes us and our experience relatable. This isn't just a book that speaks about all that you can achieve in life and ends without informing you on the all-important "how."

We, through our experiences, are an authority on what we do. This is why we are confident in guiding you through and teaching you what you need to know. OA Inc. is a company set up to help people take control of their finances with a key focus on getting people out of debt and helping them save more money, grow their income, and get to the position of early retirement.

What lies ahead are some of the most important life lessons to learn that have helped many people completely transform their lives for the better. This isn't just us saying that; we have a track record to back up our claims, too. Therefore, without further ado, it is time for you to dive into this book and learn what you came here to learn in the first place.

1

THE WORLD OF RETIREMENT

*B*efore actually retiring, you must weigh the factors that will have an influence on your retirement plans. Retirement requires strategic planning and management of your funds in such a way that you end up living the golden days. You have to take into account that planning for retirement is going to cost you time and energy, and there are a few factors to consider. We're not trying to scare you away, we are simply stating the facts that need to be understood.

First things first; if you are in debt, you need to pay it off as soon as you can. Paying off debt means collecting more and more funds for your retirement. It is as simple as it sounds, but doing so requires dedication and willpower.

People find themselves getting overwhelmed and frustrated with the burden of liabilities dangling above their heads. They tend to give up quickly and often consider themselves lost for accumulating so much debt. First off, having debt is quite normal in the U.S. You are going to have debts in one way or another at some point in your life if you are in the U.S. Whether it is credit cards or estate mortgages, it is going to involve you in itself somehow.

However, you do need to draw a line for these debts and set a limit that you are not to cross. Sure, short-term debts are somewhat easier to settle, but the long-term ones often keep you stuck and under stress for ages. Before accumulating savings or earning more, you have to make sure you do not have any sort of loan or debt on your shoulder.

So how do we start handling and paying off debts? This may sound hard, but wave goodbye to that Netflix subscription, cancel that extra gym membership that you never use, cut down on transportation costs, choose home-made over takeaways (it's healthy, too), et cetera. The more you cut your expenses, the more you start saving. With those additional few dollars, start paying extra to settle your debts quicker. In a few months, or years, you should be done with your debts.

"So I have to wait a few years in order to get started?"

Well, technically, no. We are not here to tell you to wait it out and then start. In fact, we start right now. The first phase, as you might have guessed it, is planning your retirement, knowing what your retirement is going to be like, and then reverse-engineering a plan that you can follow.

Planning is one of the most important aspects of

retirement. It is just like driving on a highway and knowing where you wish to go, the route you have to take, and so on. If you do not know this, you will never know where you are headed, or if you have made it. Unless you are aware of the goal, it is pretty daunting to figure out whether you are doing the right thing or not.

It's never too early to start thinking about retirement. Nevertheless, you should answer the following questions before deciding to quit your career:

- What is going to be the ideal age for you to retire?
- What do you plan to do when you finally retire?
- How long do you presume to live after retirement?
- What will be your source of earning when you quit?
- How long will you have to save up until retirement?
- How will you manage risks, such as inflation?

By answering these constructive questions, you will establish a clearer picture of your ultimate objective.

With that said, there are many, many other things to take into account before you decide to throw in the towel and retire.

Your Income

Oh, yes! That matters the most. What you earn deeply matters in deciding what specific amount will have to be put aside for retirement. Spending less than what you earn is a smart way to maintain your lifestyle after retirement. People are terrified to get started on dividing their income. They have a generic assumption that they may have to keep aside up to half of their earnings for savings.

The truth is, the percentage required to save is substantially lower than what you think it is. Moreover, the earlier you begin keeping that certain percentage aside, the less you are going to have to save over time. A great way to start could be by using the 50/30/20 rule.

It is as simple as it sounds: 50% of your income is to be spent on expenses and essentials to survive; 30% of your income is to be spent on your wants and desires; the remaining 20% goes aside for savings. Living on this rule might actually save you thousands of dollars every year to retire.

Time of Your Retirement

Yes, this matters as well. Deciding upon when to quit working and start relaxing is an essential part. If you do not know when you wish to stop living for life and actually live life, it tends to get challenging.

You might be a person of isolation and serenity, so you may be looking forward to retiring in your 50s and moving someplace quiet and serene. Perhaps, you are a family-loving person who wishes to retire in your early

40s to be there for your children, and maybe grandchildren, too.

You are free to choose when that time comes, but what we are pointing out here is that you need to determine the actual time of retirement, since this is going to be a big factor for your pre-retirement income that you would need to save up for. The majority of people become eligible for social security benefits earlier than retirement age. However, those benefits may increase with time if you delay your retirement, and that's a bit of a trade-off that you have to consider, too.

The earlier you choose to retire, the more savings you are going to need for your retirement income. This also means that you will become less dependent on social security, since the benefits will be lesser. In short, delaying your retirement is going to give you more advantages than you ever imagined.

Retirement Income

After you've decided on your retirement savings, you need to set a course for maintaining your current lifestyle in those golden years. You must plan for your savings to provide 45% of your pre-retirement income.

Keep in mind, the actual amount of that pre-retirement income that needs to be replaced with savings depends on a number of factors. These include your retirement age and also your anticipated retirement lifestyle. You can always hire a financial advisor to work through your plan.

You can generate your retirement income through

many ways. You can do this either by investing in retirement accounts or saving up a part of your current income.

What Do the Numbers Say?

Just over half (55%) of the Gen Yers polled claimed they have not yet begun saving for retirement. A staggering 64% indicated they do not even consider retiring. The study's most convincing finding is that Generation Y is remarkably unconcerned about retiring. According to the survey, of all non-retired generations, including Baby Boomers and Gen Xers, Gen Y is the most likely to not save. They are dubbed "Generation Procrastination" (Perman, 2011).

It stands in sharp contrast to Boomers, most of whom are Gen Y parents who are reaching retirement age and wished they had begun saving sooner. Approximately half (46%) indicated they started saving when they were 35 or older, but just one in ten currently thinks it is an appropriate age to start saving. Half of those say it's best to start saving while you're 25 or younger (Perman, 2011).

Even among Gen Yers who do have work, most are employed as freelancers or contractors, which implies no benefits–and also no job security. It's difficult to consider retiring when you don't know what will happen next year. If you do acquire a job with benefits, you may have to work for a year or be a particular age before they will begin matching whatever you put in; however, there are many hurdles for Gen Y that may be influencing their choice to save or think about retirement (Perman, 2011).

Roughly three-fourths (73%) of Gen Yers questioned believe they are not saving enough for retirement, compared to 61% of the entire population (Perman, 2011). Generation Y is the most concerned about social security running out, and the proportion of Gen Yers concerned about having to work in retirement to cover living expenses has risen from 27% to 38% in only two years (Perman, 2011).

"Building a nest egg is important, but you can't save if you're living hand to mouth" (Perman, 2011).

Money Management After Retirement

Despite your having meticulously prepared for your retirement years, you just cannot leave your personal finances on autopilot when you retire. You will still have to handle your investments, spending, and income. These may require little adjustments from time to time, or a complete revamp if your circumstance changes significantly. In this chapter, we will offer guidance on how to manage your money when you retire.

Retirement could be a prolonged process, and you may also need to make adjustments to your financial goals in the coming years. When your expenditures start to outweigh your income, there are various options for making up the difference.

Income Management

You are going to have many income streams when you retire, if you are lucky. This could be pension from a previous company, or simply income generated through retirement accounts and other assets. It may also be the social security payments or paychecks from either part-time or full-time employment.

401k or similar plans: Different regulations apply to defined contribution plans, such as a 401(k) or 403(b) plan. Investors may usually begin collecting penalty-free withdrawals from an earlier age, such as 59 and a half. There may be several circumstances, such as disabilities, which permit for earlier withdrawals.

Pension: If you have a traditional, defined-benefit pension from a previous company or labor union, you may determine when it will begin paying out income by checking the Summary Plan Description (SPD) or similar document, which the plan's administrator is obligated to furnish you with (Daugherty, 2021).

Many plans begin payments at the age of 65, but some allow you to begin receiving benefits sooner. If you haven't already decided, one essential choice you will have to make is whether to accept your payments as a single lump sum or as a number of subsequent monthly installments.

Social Security: It may be possible to start getting social security benefits before retiring. However, you do need to be at least 62 years old in order to do that. You can also retire first and collect your social security afterwards. In any case, if you have retired and not yet claimed social security, you will have to decide when you need your payments to begin.

Other Investments: Other than the above three, you may as well withdraw funds from your non-retirement accounts at any age or time. And you do not even have to worry about the RMDs. It would be advantageous for you to time these withdrawals to coincide with your other income sources.

Job Income (if you are working): You should keep in mind that if you plan to work in your retirement, it may have an effect on your social security benefits. If you are earning more than a certain amount before reaching full retirement, for every $2 you earn over the yearly limit, social security will lower your monthly income by $1 (Daugherty, 2021).

Investment Management

Apart from any considerations regarding drawing on your assets for income, you must keep a watch over how your money is invested and possibly make several necessary adjustments along the journey.

As they get older, retirees frequently shift to more traditional, less risky asset allocations, focusing more on protecting their money rather than increasing it. For instance, a typical rule of thumb proposes that people subtract their age from 110 to estimate the amount of capital to invest in equities. Applying that criterion, a 65-year-old retiree may target 45% stock and 55% bond asset allocation, with the latter being regarded as less hazardous. At the age of 75, the retiree will have switched to 35% equities and 65% bonds, and so on.

There are always other options, such as mutual funds and other investments that can do it for you. However, if you are opting to adjust asset allocation on your own, keep in mind the consequences of taxes.

Expense Management

In any case, if you find yourself in a situation where

your retirement income is not sufficient and your expenses are greater, you can always increase one and decrease the other. Expenses is the part that you will mostly have control over.

Since housing expenditures constitute a significant portion of most people's budgets, it is a smart thing to start with. For instance, you could consider relocating to an area with a lower cost of living. Or how about staying in your existing neighborhood but downsizing to a smaller, less costly home?

Your insurance costs can also be reduced as an option. You might not need insurance plans if you have children who are independent. If you own a couple of cars but you do not need one, you can also save up on auto insurance along with repair costs and maintenance by selling one.

Budgeting for the Four Phases of Retirement

Now, physical factors count in your retirement if you want a secure and long-lasting one. If you are healthy and financially prepared, your retirement will last longer than you anticipate. However, your retirement will be going through different phases. Such as was mentioned before, the fluctuation in income and expenses will require budgeting over time.

Even if you are opting for a shorter retirement, the phases will be pretty much the same. Experts like to call these phases different names or sometimes number them differently. These phases are:

. . .

PRE-RETIREMENT AGE *(AGE 50 or Under)*

Pre-retirement is basically the time when you are just about to retire. You might yet be working but also approaching retirement. You are finally able to see the bigger and clearer picture about what and how your expenses, income, and nest egg will look. Along with that, you are also capable of figuring out precisely what you will be doing after retirement.

Usually, the end of this phase is considered at age 62, since this is the time when people start qualifying for social security. Many folks retire by 55 or so; meanwhile, others tend to work well into their 70s.

In this phase, you need to figure out what your source of income will be, how your social security will be paid out, how much you have invested in retirement accounts, and how much you will be able to withdraw each month from those balances.

Beginning of Retirement *(Age 62 and Above)*

Your life is going to go through major changes and evolutions in this phase. You have finally retired. However, you do not have those steady paychecks coming into your account anymore, aside from any pension that you may have. You will need to strategize your income and spending plan in this phase.

Moreover, you can also begin claiming your social security benefits at this age. Losing your employer-sponsored medical insurance is one thing. Therefore, make sure you have a solid coverage or backup plan for you and your better half or any other person dependent on you.

The interesting part about this phase is that you will

feel tempted to go on a spending spree. Having lots of leisure time and perhaps having promised yourself an exotic vacation, you may feel the itch to spend more than anticipated. If you have set your budget and it permits you, then go on a trip and have the time of your life. However, be careful not to end up spending all of your savings!

One way to keep things under control, such as managing new expenses and easing the drain on your savings, is to have some more income. This entails seeking part-time employment or even going for seasonal jobs.

Furthermore, since your employment no longer binds you to a certain area, this may be the ideal moment to relocate. Moving might be a financial boon—or a significant belt tightener—depending on the standard of living where you presently live versus where you want to go.

Mid Retirement (70 to 80)

By this time or age, you will already be enjoying whatever you had planned for yourself. This could include profit from your investment or social security benefits. However, take note that no financial incentive is to be delayed after this age.

You should begin drawing standard minimum distributions from several types of retirement funds at the age of 72, including 401(k), profit sharing, 457(b), 403(b), Roth 401(k) plans, and even the majority of IRAs (but not Roth IRAs). If you are not in any investment that automatically adjusts your asset allocation, as in a target date fund, now is an excellent moment to do so.

You may also experience a reduction in your expenditures at this point, in addition to receiving some extra revenue. You might wish to be traveling less and spending more time at home, or you might prefer to focus your travel on less expensive visits to see grandkids and perhaps other friends or relatives. Hopefully, your children will have progressed far enough in their jobs that they will no longer need you for financial support. Moreover, you might no longer require life insurance.

Late Retirement (80 and Above)

The most financially concerning thing by this time might be your medical expenses, since this is the age of health deterioration. You are going to have out-of-pocket expenditures for stuff like deductibles and co-payments; however, Medicare will likely cover the majority of them.

Also, your expenses might turn out to be the same as middle retirement. Many of the older folks consider moving to nursing homes or senior care centers, but the choice is entirely up to you for this decision.

You might wish to reevaluate your retirement resources at this time to determine if they are sufficient to carry you through. Unless you find yourself short on cash but still living in your house, you are going to have the option of exploring a reverse mortgage as a means of finance. When considering how much you have left, contemplate how you would like to live your days and whatever you wish to leave to others, including any charitable intentions.

Should You Retire Within the U.S. or Elsewhere?

Let's be honest. There are many of us who may have actually given this a bit of thought, and it's perfectly okay if you did.

Countless issues arise when it comes to retirement planning: When should I retire? How much money should I set aside? Will I keep working and/or volunteering? What shall I do to keep myself occupied? One element that determines how you respond to these issues is whether you plan on retiring in the United States or overseas.

While the majority of Americans choose to spend their retirement in the United States, an increasing number of people are deciding to retire abroad. To give you some ideas, let's talk about the perks and challenges a person may face while deciding where to retire.

Retiring in the U.S.

A whopping majority of retirees opt to remain in their current residences or relocate within the state. Family is a key motivator for a lot of folks to live in their current location, particularly if there are grandchildren in the picture. Well, the decision hangs entirely on you, but we can list a few pros and cons for you to consider:

Pros:

- Professional relationships are already formed. These could assist you in finding a part-time or less demanding full-time job once you retire.
- Social networks are already developed. You

could stay physically and intellectually engaged without having to make new acquaintances.

- You have a family. It gets a lot easier when you have blood ties around you.
- You have support. You are not surrounded by strangers at all, you know everyone around you.
- Providers you can trust. You will be able to continue seeing your regular physicians and hospitals, as well as hair/body groomers and vehicle mechanics.
- You have convenience and stability. Anything from transportation to the kind of shampoo offered at your local supermarket has a certain amount of dependability.
- You have your comfort zone. You can be content with your "certain" routine.

Cons:

- Same routine. Even though some may consider this a perk, always having the same routine may limit your ability to enjoy and have new experiences.
- It is expensive. Living in the U.S. entails a much higher cost of living than in other countries.
- Costs of assisted living are quite high. You might not need it, though according to

Genworth's Cost of Care Survey, the average expense of community and assisted living facilities in the United States is $4,300 per month (Folger, 2021).

- Costs of healthcare are escalating. Although the quality of service is good, the expense of healthcare is high. According to estimates, a healthy 65-year-old couple retiring in the United States in 2019 will require $606,337 in healthcare costs (Folger, 2021).

Retiring Abroad

Relocating out of the nation is obviously exciting; however, the level of excitement varies depending on your location. You might select a location that meets your satisfaction level in terms of contemporary comforts, accessibility, weather, hobbies, cuisine, medical, social, and traditions, ranging from calm beaches in Vietnam to hip cities in South America.

But here's the thing. You get to enjoy new experiences and learn new opportunities that may bring a level of contentment to you which you haven't experienced yet. Let's go over the pros and cons of retiring abroad as well:

Pros:

- Achieve your ambitions. You could fulfill your desires to explore, learn a different sport, or pursue a pastime.
- New encounters. New experiences, according to experts, are linked to good aging because

they give physical, intellectual, and social advantages (Folger, 2021).

- Medical at a reasonable cost. Public health providers that give proper care at an affordable price can be found. Many nations provide private insurance at a lower cost than equivalent policies in the United States. Conventional Medicare doesn't quite support healthcare costs outside of the United States, while some Medicare Advantage plans do.

- Incentives of a retiree. Many nations provide pensioners with incentives, such as Panama's Pensionado scheme, which gives discounts on everything from meals and drinks to movies for seniors who fulfill modest minimum income requirements (Folger, 2021).

- Reasonable living cost. Retiring abroad may help you live at a much more reasonable cost of living than that of the U.S. This is going to be really helpful if you are tight on the budgeting end.

- Different weather. You could enjoy completely different weather and experience seasons like never before.

Cons:

- Far away from home. Even though you have many facilities, you are still far away from home and you might miss it from time to time.

- Visas that may be long stays. Certain nations welcome international retirees and provide a straightforward road to stay, whereas others provide no retirement visa options.
- Taxation times two. The United States taxes its residents' earnings regardless of where they reside. You would have to pay taxes on your earnings in both the United States and overseas, based on wherever you choose to retire. Although most nations do not impose double taxes on retirees, you could still be required to submit returns with both of them.
- Differences between language and culture. Are you fascinated by learning another language and experiencing a different culture? Might be a big no from your side.
- Not too stable. It is not like every country has the same economic stability as the United States.
- Every day brings new problems. It is possible that the commodities, services, and comforts you're used to won't be easily available.
- The difference between vacationing and living. Your bit of heaven might be lovely to explore, but not so attractive to live in forever.
- Social support. If anything ever turns out badly, you could find yourself among strangers.

A lot of retirees would never contemplate going overseas, while others are certain it is their dream. If that's the case, start preparing early, because getting your paper-work and logistics in place might take months, years, or even longer than that.

Whether you're a retiree or someone who is close to being retired and undecided, you must do some self-examination to find your true soul. Perhaps a trip overseas (possibly multiple) might be good to test the waters prior to making any big decisions.

Countries to Consider for Retirement

A relocation overseas could be the ticket if you want to push your retirement savings even further. Life in a different country allows you to explore more of the globe while also lowering your living expenses. But what other nations are the greatest for retirees?

Annually, International Living's Annual Global Retirement Index ranks the finest nations for retirees, and the top ten list for 2021 includes five Spanish-speaking countries in Central and South America. If you're thinking of retiring to another country, studying Spanish could be a good idea (Lake, 2021).

International Living employs a rating methodology that considers many characteristics to decide which nations are the greatest for retirees, which include:

1. Renting Cost
2. Living expenses
3. Country's political situation and stability
4. The ease of purchasing and holding real estate, as well as the value of property investments

5. Facilities and support for things such as medical and entertainment
6. Requirements of visa along with residency
7. Social fitting and how challenging it is to adjust to the crowd
8. Buildings and infrastructure
9. Healthiness
10. Climate
11. Amenities and entertainment

The following are the top five countries that have the highest cumulative average score in all of those factors:

Costa Rica

If you appreciate an active and healthy lifestyle, Costa Rica is going to be an excellent option. It achieved high results in the areas of medical, infrastructure, and government, although there's plenty to see and do. Costa Rica's low cost of living makes it accessible to even the most modest retirement budget.

Panama

Panama gives retirees the best of both worlds, with stunning mountains and lively beaches. Locals are known for being kind and polite, and the living costs are quite cheap. Almost everything is cheaper in comparison to the United States, including restaurants, rent, and groceries.

Mexico

Mexico blends contemporary conveniences with such a country vibe, making it ideal for retirees who desire a warm temperature and closeness to the United States. On International Living's list, it received the greatest score including both facilities and entertainment, as well as the simplicity of acquiring a residence.

Colombia

Whether you enjoy the mountains, the beach, or even exploring the rainforest, Colombia has it all. There are lots of nonstop flights between Florida to almost any big Colombian city, which is a cool combination of colonial and urban. Retirement visas are easy to get if you can provide evidence of retirement money; however, they must be updated every three years.

Portugal

Portugal is among the three European countries represented in the top ten. People are drawn to this seaside European location due to the obvious inexpensive cost of living and plenty of facilities, in addition to the gorgeous scenery.

The best part is that English is being taught in schools, making it easier for Americans to converse with the locals. There seem to be countless islands to explore, plus the cheap and diverse restaurant selection makes it a foodie's heaven. Portugal received top marks in cost of living, housing, climate, and healthcare.

2

PLANNING FOR RETIREMENT

*I*n the previous chapter, we discussed how the current generation is neglecting and, more precisely, ignoring the importance of planning for retirement, though this is undoubtedly a crucial priority to consider. Your job is done, your career has come to an end, and you have no purpose in life–now what? The answer to this very question is the concept and reality of retirement.

The good part is, you possess the power to make your retirement worthwhile. And that starts now. Planning for your retirement is a multi-step procedure that is going to evolve with time. You will need to build yourself a financial cushion to enjoy the comfort, fun, and security part of retirement.

Determining time horizons, predicting expenditures, calculating necessary after-tax returns, measuring risk profile, and completing estate planning are all important aspects of retirement planning. To leverage the power of compounding, make preparations for retirement as soon as possible.

Young investors might be able to afford taking greater risks in investments, whilst those nearing retirement need to be more cautious. Portfolios should be rebalanced and estate plans revised as appropriate when retirement plans change over time.

Get to Know Your Time Horizon

The primary foundation of a successful retirement strategy is laid by your present age and predicted retirement age. The more time you have between now and retirement, the more risk your portfolio can bear. Young investors who have more than 30 years to retire should have a majority of their assets in risky investments (like stocks). Stocks have traditionally beaten other products, such as bonds, over lengthy periods of time, despite the fact that there will be fluctuation. The key word here seems to be "long," which means at least ten years.

To keep balance in your purchasing power, you need to have returns that outpace inflation. Compound growth on money is something we have all heard about, and it is something we all want. Inflation, on the other hand, is a form of 'compound anti-growth,' as it diminishes the value of your money.

Over 24 years, a low inflation rate of 3% will destroy the value of your investments by 50% (Pinkasovitch, 2020).

It may not seem like a lot per year, but over time, it adds up to a significant amount.

It might be hard to believe that a small amount of money saved now will matter considerably in your twenties; however, compounding could turn that money into a much larger number by the time you need to use it.

Generally speaking, as you get older, your portfolio needs to be more concerned with income and capital safety. This implies putting more money into assets like bonds, which is not going to provide you with the same returns as that of stocks but rather would be less risky and give you extra income you can survive on. You would be somewhat less worried about inflation as well.

Breaking up your retirement planning into multiple elements will prove to be advantageous for you. Let's assume that a parent wishes to retire in a couple of years. They wish to pay for their child's education at the age of 18 and further wish to relocate to Florida. As for a retirement planning perspective, their strategy would be broken into three parts:

1. Two years until retirement (contributions must still be made)
2. Saving up and paying for college
3. Relocating to Florida (frequent withdrawals to cover living expenses)

To identify the best allocation approach, a multi-stage retirement plan must take into account varied time horizons as well as the related liquidity demands. Your investments must also be rebalanced throughout periods as your time horizon shifts.

Figure Out How Much Money You Will Need

Predicting realistically for post-retirement expense habits will allow you to figure an accurate and satisfactory size for a retirement portfolio. The majority of people believe that their spending might reduce by 70 to 80% after retiring, which is very unrealistic. Such cases are proved to be faulty when unexpected medical expenses show up or the mortgages have not been paid in full.

"I feel that the ratio should be closer to 100% for retirees to have enough funds for retirement," says David G. Niggel, CFP, ChFC, AIF, who is founder, president, and CEO of Key Ialth Partners, LLC in Lititz. "Every year, the cost of living rises, particularly healthcare costs. People are living longer and want to make the most of their retirement years. Retirees will require greater income for a longer period of time; therefore, they must save and invest properly" (Pinkasovitch, 2020).

Because retirees are no longer required to work for eight hours or more every day, they have more leisure time to sightsee, shop, travel, and partake in other costly pastimes. More spending in the future necessitates extra savings today; thus, accurate retirement spending expectations contribute to the planning process.

It is critical to have an accurate estimate of your retirement costs, since it will determine how often you withdraw annually along with how you fund your account.

You can swiftly outlive your portfolio if you understate your spending, and if you exaggerate your expenses, you risk not being able to enjoy the retirement lifestyle you choose.

Furthermore, if you plan to buy a house or finance your child's education after retirement, you may need more money than you anticipate. These expenses must be considered in the comprehensive retirement strategy. Keep in mind that you should review your plan now and then to ensure that you are in line with your savings.

Compute the After-Tax Rate of Returns on Investments

Once you have determined the projected time horizons and expenditure obligations, you need to calculate the after-tax real rate of return to evaluate the portfolio's ability to provide the required earnings. Even for long-term investing, a required rate of return of more than ten percent (before taxes) is usually unreasonable. Because low-risk retirement portfolios generally consist of low-yielding fixed-income assets, this returns criterion decreases as you become older.

Investment returns are usually taxed based on the sort of retirement plan you have. As a result, the real rate of return should be computed after taxes. Assessing your tax position once you start withdrawing cash, on the other hand, is an important part of the retirement planning process.

Examine Your Risk Tolerance in Relation to Your Investment Objectives

A correct portfolio allocation that balances the worries of risk aversion plus return targets is likely the most crucial stage in retirement planning; either you or a skilled financial consultant should be in control of the investment selections. How much risk are you prepared to accept in order to achieve your goals? Should a portion of your earnings be invested in risk-free treasury bonds to cover necessary expenses?

You must be satisfied with the risks you are willing to take for your portfolio and understand the difference between necessities and luxuries. You also need to discuss this with your family along with the financial advisor, since this is a crucial part for everyone.

When your portfolio's numerous mutual funds have a difficult year, try adding extra money to them. That is just like parenthood: the kid who requires your affection most often is the one who deserves it the least. Portfolios have a lot in common with parenting. Do not sell the mutual fund you're upset with this year because it may be the greatest performer next year.

An Eye Over Estate Planning

Another important element in a well-prepared retirement plan is estate planning, but each aspect requires the skills of various experts in that discipline, such as attorneys and accountants. Life insurance is indeed a crucial component of estate retirement planning and an estate plan.

Developing a comprehensive estate plan and life insurance coverage guarantees that your assets are transferred according to your preferences and that your family members are not financially disadvantaged when you pass away. A well-thought-out plan can also help you avoid costly and time-consuming court proceedings.

Another important aspect of estate preparation is tax planning. If a person ends up leaving property to family or a charity, the tax consequences of either gifting or transferring the property through the estate procedures must still be evaluated.

The goal of a popular retirement plan investing strategy involves providing returns that cover annual inflation-adjusted lifestyle expenditures whilst also maintaining the portfolio's value. The portfolio is subsequently passed on to the deceased's heirs. To identify the best solution for the person, you should speak with a tax adviser.

Striking a balance between realistic returns expectations and desired standard of living is one of the most challenging parts while developing a comprehensive retirement plan. The best thing you can do is to begin a flexible portfolio that can be evolved and updated with the changing times.

Early Retirement

Early retirement generally means a person's exit from work before the age of 65 or so. This age also entails that Americans are now fully eligible for Medicare. Of course, when you are trying something out of the ordinary, it requires extraordinary effort, too. Retiring early is something like that. Not everyone wishes to retire and relax, but those who do are quite passionate about it.

The passionate ones are only a few. However, some unlucky folks are forced to retire due to uncertain and unfortunate circumstances. For instance, they are met with devastating accidents that may disqualify their bodies from working. They are forced to retire in such a state because, what can they do in the end next to nothing, right?

I recommend that you be smart enough to be well-prepared for your retirement if by chance you are met with such circumstances. Early retirement issues may be overcome by cutting back on spending, planning your money, and making wise financial decisions, regardless of your position.

Is it possible to retire early?

Many U.S. citizens find it daunting to retire early. However, doing so requires thorough planning and strategic moves to ensure financial stability throughout.

Employees of civil service or members of the military are the usual ones to retire early. They have often been subjected to retirement with full pensions and medical facilities even before the age of 65. Those people who work in rather higher earning industries and make a sizable revenue are likely to be saving more in their early careers.

But, how do I retire early?

Easy peasy lemon squeezy... not really. Early retirement demands out-of-the-way sacrifices. However, to begin with, you need to set realistic goals for your retirement. Again, seeing yourself on Miami Beach with a lavish estate and a shiny BMW is nothing but an elusive wish.

If you plan to retire at a young age, you have got to maintain passive income streams such as earning service charges through freelance consultation or profitable investments. You are going to have to restrict expenditures if you are to retire before 65.

If you really want to retire but do not want to give up working, you can opt for semi-retirement. This is a concept of doing entrepreneurial business rather than a nine-to-five job. You still work and generate revenue, but not through working in a traditional environment. Sounds great, right?

For the next part, you should be planning for an annual budget. Look, traveling around the globe is going to cost you greatly and require living on a tight budget or even a frugal lifestyle. You can begin by evaluating your current expenses. To have the most reasonable budget plan, go through at least a year's worth of your account statements and credit card details. Categorize each and every purchase and take into account which ones are unnecessary. Chop them off like they are your worst nightmare.

With these little tips and tricks, you may end up saving enough to retire earlier than usual. Enjoying life with financial stability and comfortable retirement is going to feel like heaven.

Retirement Lifestyle

Retirement is not only about financial stability. Your lifestyle plays a major role in your retirement planning.

You need to think about how you wish to live as a retiree regarding your retirement funds. In your old age, what sort of lifestyle would fit you best?

What do you want to accomplish when you retire? Do you want to follow the crowd, or do you want to forge your own path? Do you want to unwind or do you want to be as busy as possible? Your retirement plans should aim to provide financial stability as well as emotional and physical well-being.

You can, for example, spend time with the grandkids and just enjoy being a grandparent if it suits you. If you want to start a new job, perhaps consulting or selling your crafts might be a good fit. Alternatively, you may simply enjoy yourself by playing tennis or putting a hammock on the beachfront.

Sometimes retirees like jogging to the track, gardening, or working on home improvement projects. There is always the alternative of traveling. Others may find volunteering or returning to school to be very fulfilling.

Most importantly, you need to ensure that your health is up to the mark and quite stable. Experts suggest staying active and quitting smoking along with drinking if you wish a longer, healthier life.

Researchers followed up with 4,497 individuals 22.6 years after they answered a population-based health survey, and their findings were published in PLOS ONE in July 2019. At the time of the study (2006–2008), the average age of respondents was 52.7 years (Silvestrini, 2021).

The following lifestyle factors of effective aging were discovered by the researchers:

- Physical Activity
- Alcohol
- Obesity
- Smoking
- Social support

According to studies from the University of Exeter Medical School in the U.K., maintaining a healthy lifestyle reduces the risk of dementia among cognitively healthy older persons (Silvestrini, 2021).

Unusual Lifestyles

Perhaps you might not enjoy golfing or spending time with your grandchildren. You perhaps prefer to live an unorthodox retirement lifestyle. You might want to spend the rest of your life aboard a cruise ship. You won't be the first older citizen who chooses to live on a sailing ship.

Perhaps you have always been drawn to the broader picture. You might acquire a trucker license and head out of town, earning money while seeing the country. There are already unique retirement communities for folks who have common interests like astronomy or art forms. People who travel by water or aircraft might also find communities of like-minded people.

Estate Planning

Your estate is made up of everything you possess, such as your property, bank accounts, stamp collection, vinyl record collections, art, or vehicles. To ensure that you have a role in how your fortune is allocated, estate planning is vital. This might appear difficult or challenging at first, but a little effort today can provide a huge benefit to your family members later and will potentially spare them big bucks.

Conversely, if you put off putting your estate plan in place, you might find yourself in a scenario where you are unable to enforce paperwork owing to illness or fatality. Start planning now from this detailed step-by-step estate planning guide.

1. *Make a list of your assets*–this way you acknowledge your net worth.
2. *Seek professional assistance*–to ensure everything is done legally.
3. *Prepare a will and nominate beneficiaries*–so that your estate is secured within a family.
4. *Seek to establish a living trust*–to remove the necessity of probate.
5. *Compile records for retirement accounts*–such as IRAs and 401(k)s, and double-check beneficiary preferences.
6. *Compile annuity statements.*
7. *Verify that almost all company interests are taken into consideration* and that the ownership structure is understood.
8. *Make a list of any furniture, literature, family heirlooms, valuable jewelry, or other items.*

When you have completed your inventory, you will

have to pose to yourself a crucial question. Which items and possessions will you wish to keep or pass on to others when you pass away? Evaluate what you possess on your own and with your partner. After that, make a list of intended recipients or individuals who will acquire these assets.

You will have to assess the worth of both intangible and tangible assets; therefore, a recent property valuation of your house as well as other goods will come in handy. In other circumstances, though, a precise figure isn't required, and a "best guess" estimate will suffice.

Options for Your Retirement Accounts

Well over a dozen various sorts of retirement savings programs are regulated by the Internal Revenue Service. Any of these options could be beneficial for you, based on your situation and eligibility. Or, you can invest in an annuity to ensure a steady stream of income throughout retirement.

Let's talk about the most common ones here to help you find what is best for you:

401(k) Account

Employees can contribute a percentage of their income to a retirement savings account through 401(k) plans offered by many businesses. Several companies will even match a fraction of your contributions.

Contributions to a 401(k) are eligible for tax deduction, and the money invested in the account can accumulate tax-deferred. Withdrawals are taxed, on the other hand.

The contribution maximum for 401(k) plans is $19,500 as of 2021. You may potentially contribute $6,500 in 401(k) catch-up contributions if you are 50 or older, bringing your total 401(k) contributions to $25,500 (Silvestrini, 2021b).

Within the context of retirement savings, 401(k) plans have a series of benefits and pitfalls. Learning the benefits and drawbacks of various retirement plans will assist with making financial decisions while you plan for retirement.

If you look at the brighter side, you will be privileged with Federal protection under ERISA–Employee Retirement Income Security Act. By that law, your retirement plan money shall be protected by standards set for employers.

However, the challenges you face might include limited investments, account fees, and penalties. It is crucial to seek advice from a financial counsellor who is experienced with your specific situation as you assess the benefits and drawbacks. Expanding your investment portfolios and utilizing several retirement sources of income, such as annuities, can help you optimize your savings.

Individual Retirement Account (IRAs)

IRAs are a convenient method that can save money. You could open an account to routinely take money from the savings fund as well as transfer it into your IRA. IRAs sometimes offer tax benefits. Whenever you register the IRA, you will get a couple of choices—a standard IRA or perhaps a Roth IRA. Whichever choice you make will determine how your payments and withdrawals are taxed.

Deposits to the typical IRA, for instance, are tax-deductible. Contributions to a Roth IRA are not tax-deductible. An IRA allows you to contribute up to $6,000 each year. The maximum is $7,000 per year if you are 50 or above. These restrictions apply to all of your conventional and Roth IRA accounts together. Rollover contributions from some other retirement accounts are not subject to the limitations.

You were not allowed to make deposits into a conventional IRA after the age of 70 and a half until the legislation changed in 2020 (Silvestrini, 2021b). And you were required to begin withdrawing, termed as mandated minimum distributions, at that age.

Nonetheless, starting in 2021, you are able to contribute to your IRA at any time or age. The new regulation delays the start of required minimum payouts until the age of 72. This only refers to those people who turn 70 and a half after the year 2019. Those who turn that age in 2019 or earlier must adhere to the prior standards (Silvestrini, 2021b).

If you're still employed at 72 and do not own more than 5% of the company you work for, then you are eligible to defer drawing RMDs from your employer's plan unless you retire, according to the new regulation (Silvestrini, 2021b).

Roth IRAs

Contributions to a Roth IRA are not deductible for tax purposes. The perk seems to be that withdrawals are thereafter tax-free. You may also contribute to a Roth IRA when you are above 70 and a half years old. Likewise, withdrawals from a Roth account are not mandatory at any given age.

If withdrawals from Roth funds are considered qualifying distributions, they are not taxed. The withdrawal should indeed take place within five years after the account was opened and the first deposit was made to be regarded as a qualified distribution.

However, you do need to fulfil the following conditions in order to be considered eligible:

- Must be at least 59 and a half years old
- Must be disabled
- Must be the beneficiary of a Roth owner who is not alive anymore
- After your death, a beneficiary of your estate makes the withdrawal
- You, your spouse, or your partner's offspring, parent, grandchild, or any other ancestor received up to $10,000 to build, buy, or repair the first home

You may be subject to a 10% tax penalty for early withdrawals if the money is not considered a qualifying distribution (Silvestrini, 2021b). While you approach retirement, you might also want to explore converting your IRA or 401(k) into an annuity for your retirement income to be driven by converted savings.

Annuities

Whenever you retire, a retirement annuity makes it

possible to have a source of income that will last your entire life. An income annuity, or annuitized annuity, protects from certain longevity risks, retirement risks, or the threat of outliving your funds. They provide the exact tax advantages just like other retirement plans in that they accumulate tax-deferred until the investments are withdrawn.

401(k) programs might presently include annuities in their programs. However, only a few firms do so, owing to legal difficulties with the insurance companies that offer annuities. Companies that accept annuities as part of their programs will be protected by legislation.

Difference Between 401(k)s and IRAs

Some folks are terrified or perplexed by the prospect of investing. These appear to be a plethora of queries, such as "Do I choose a 401k or an IRA?" or "Which investment products could I deposit in?" Putting these back for a moment, the key thing is to make a habit of saving money, even if it is a small amount, for retirement purposes. Then put those savings in equities or bonds. Which ultimately means, do not even set up an IRA with cash in CDs.

Let's weigh the differences between 401ks and IRAs now that this has been explained.

- 401(k) is an employer-sponsored account while IRA is for individual purposes.
- 401(k)'s annual contribution limit is $19,000 while IRA implies a limit of $5,500 only.
- 401(k) have no income limits while IRA does imply limits.
- 401(k) investment options are limited by plan

but IRA applies no limit for investment options.

- 401(k) can be rarely cashed out without penalty whereas IRA can sometimes be cashed out penalty-free.

Everyone's decision to invest in a 401(k) or an IRA is unique and is influenced by a variety of factors. 401(k)s are indeed the simplest way to save enough for retirement for individuals who are qualified. Limited investment options might be beneficial, since they streamline investing selections and funds are automatically deducted from your paycheck.

Several companies will match a portion or most of your 401(k) investments up to a specified amount. You should contribute to a 401(k) plan if your work provides one and you are qualified. You're squandering free money if they provide a plan with matching contributions and you do not take advantage of it.

Assuming you do not have any accessibility to a 401(k), or if yours has been exceeded out and yet you still have to save for retirement, an IRA is a good option. If you are interested, there are also a number of socially responsible and tech-focused funds to choose from.

3

INVESTMENT STRATEGIES FOR
RETIREMENT

One cannot simply retire without upping their game with analytical strategies. And this doesn't just apply to retirement; each and every goal you set requires strategic moves and smart steps along the way to be successful. If you want to play it smart while you are planning your retirement, you need to pick your strategies wisely.

Planning for retirement might well be daunting, particularly if you feel you are starting late or off track. According to a Federal Reserve assessment on the financial well-being of U.S. families released in 2019, just 44% aged 45–59 believed their retirement savings were on course, leaving 56% adrift (Weliver, 2021).

We have broken down these strategies into three parts:

1. Paying off debts
2. Choosing the right investments

3. Managing your portfolios

Just as we mentioned in the introductory part of this book, paying off your debts is the most crucial part. We are strong believers that it is simply not easy or possible to save a greater amount of funds for your retirement if you have debts to be paid. There are many ways to get rid of debt as soon as possible; these strategies are not only important and crucial to the process but they are also convenient.

Bid Farewell to Your Debts

The truth is, if you are to say goodbye to your liabilities, it is going to take some willpower on your part. It is not just about transferring your money here and there. It is more linked with your mental state and impulses. If you think you are not strong enough to overcome your emotions and start taking steps toward productive things, you need to change that.

Build yourself into such a rational human that no emotion gets a chance to throw you off track. Emotions play a great part in every aspect of life; therefore, they might get tangled in your financial life as well. Once you have built yourself up with such strong nerves, you can start leaping towards a successful life and contented retirement.

Here are a few tips to overcome your debts.

- **Compile all of your debt, bills, and loans**

Before deciding how to pay off your debts, start by analyzing and compiling each and every bill or loan that is liable to you. You will have to go through your credit card and bank statements for the past six months or so.

You will get a list of all the monthly payments, expenses, interest rates or terms, and a total balance along with all the relevant details. For instance, you will take into account if any of the bills are currently in deferment or in a special repayment plan.

- **Try paying more than the minimum payment**

Have a look at your budget and try to see if something can be squeezed out to make room for a few extra dollars. When you pay more than the minimum requirement, you eventually end up saving on interest, and this will help you get out of your debt sooner.

- **Try debt snowball**

If you are paying more than the minimum required amount, you can give the snowball debt method a shot. This loan repayment technique requires you to pay the bare minimum on almost all of your liabilities besides the lowest, on which you should pay as much as possible. You may swiftly pay off your smallest debt by "snowballing" amounts toward it, then moving on to the next lowest liability while making minimum payments on the others.

This method motivates you to focus on a single debt at a time. This should ultimately help you stay on track and maintain momentum along the way. However, in the case of a payday loan or title loan, disregard the snowball method since they have a much higher rate of interest.

- **Try refinancing your debts**

Debt refinancing to a reasonable interest rate should save you big bucks in interest while also allowing you to pay off your debt quickly. Auto loans, personal loans, student loans, and mortgages may all be refinanced.

A debt consolidation loan, which is a personal loan with a lower rate of interest than your previous loans, is one method you can use to achieve this. You might want to consider switching credit card debt to a balance transfer card if you have credit card debt.

- **Use windfalls to pay off debts**

Rather than storing the money in your bank account or overspending on yourself, allocate it to your loans when you get a tax return or bonus check. You have the option of devoting the full windfall to debt or dividing it 50/50 between loans and something rewarding, such as a future getaway or a lavish supper.

- **Accept a settlement that is less than what you owe**

You could also contact your creditors and arrange a debt relief, generally for a far lower amount than you need to pay. Although you may do it personally, there are a number of third-party firms that offer debt settlement services for a price.

Saving for Retirement

We do not believe that we need to overemphasize the importance of savings at every age. However, you need to save more than you invest. This is because relying on pensions and social security won't provide you with the lifestyle that you have dreamed of. As a matter of fact, we believe more than 45% of the retirement earnings need to be sourced from your savings.

That is exactly why we recommend you save more or less 15% of your pre-tax household income. Regardless of whether saving that exact amount is just not possible, inquire whether your company has a program that automatically advances contributions every year until a target is achieved.

A further way to get started is by paying enough to match an employer match, and contributing all or some of any raises or yearly bonuses to your employment savings account or independent retirement fund until you hit the annual contribution limit.

Short-Term Saving Strategy

Almost everybody knows to keep an emergency fund. You are a risk-taker if you do not prepare an emergency fund for yourself. Unfortunate events never inform you beforehand. They are always a surprise, and as you probably already know, a frustrating one. It could be anything, such as losing your job or facing an illness or even having met with an accident.

Emergency does not come knocking at your door, so you should always have a backup plan. That's where the savings part comes in. Having enough put aside to cover approximately three to six months of necessary expenditures is generally a good rule of thumb. Consider this emergency fund as necessary bill payment and commit to it until you have set aside enough.

Although emergency reserves are intended to cover more serious situations such as loss of employment, we also recommend setting aside a certain amount of your earnings to handle lesser unanticipated expenditures. Who has never been asked to at least one celebration? Have a shattered screen on your mobile phone? Got in the car to find a flat tire? Furthermore, there are several costs that are frequently forgotten, such as automobile upkeep and maintenance, family outings for children, prescription expenses for medical visits, Halloween costumes, or even Christmas gifts, to name a few.

One thing that can help with these one-time expenses is to set aside 5% of your monthly earnings. It is undoubtedly a great idea to put aside a few bucks for these expenses instead of taking money from emergency funds. How do you get this 5% of your earnings? The above target can be met by having money routinely deducted from a paycheck and placed in a separate account designated solely for short-term savings.

Our recommendations are meant to be a basic foundation. It is vital to assess your circumstances and make any required adjustments to these recommendations. You're doing a fantastic job if you're near the 50/15/5 saving and spending goal. Here are a few more suggestions: Pay off high-interest debt first. You might save the leftover money for other purposes, such as financing for a kid's education or wedding. Ultimately, putting money into retirement savings will make logical sense for folks who wish to retire early or have not really been saving regularly.

The best part is that it is not simply keeping track of every dime. Monitoring your present saving and spending habits in light of our three areas will help you gain authority and, more precisely, confidence. The financial condition of just about everyone will alter throughout time. Cash flow may be affected by marriage, a new job, children, or another lifestyle factor. It is a smart option to review your saving and spending habits on a frequent basis, especially following major milestones.

Maximizing Your Retirement Savings

You can maximize your retirement savings by doing small stuff. They may seem like small things, but they can actually be quite significant. To have a happy retirement, according to Fidelity Investments, you should have saved the equivalent of 10 times your annual salary by the age of 67. Based on the typical American salary statistics from the U.S. Bureau of Labor Statistics, this equates to around $544,440 in savings, and many experts suggest you will need at least $1 million (DeMatteo, 2020).

It might be intimidating to think of saving half a

million dollars or more, but experts recommend setting modest savings goals throughout your life. According to the rule of thumb, by the age of 30, you should have the equivalent of one year's income in the bank, which would be around $40,508 based on typical U.S. wages (DeMatteo, 2020).

If you have been falling behind on your retirement savings, we have got some advice to help you get back on track.

- **Savings Rate Matters**

To make up for the shortfall, we recommend focusing on your savings rate first. According to experts, prior to the age of 25, you can save 15% of your income and be well on your way to retirement (DeMatteo, 2020). Using a percentage instead of a monetary number implies that if your income increases, your savings should increase as well.

However, if you begin saving at the age of 30, you will have lost out on five years of savings as well as all of the money you might have collected. In order to keep up, you will really have to consider saving more than 15% of your income. Begin immediately, invest whatever you can afford right now, and be persistent.

- **Stay Away From Lifestyle Inflation**

There's still time to come back if you have only begun saving in your 30s. This would be the year to throw your career into full force and look for chances and upgrades that will help you go from basic-level to secure incomes. You may boost your savings as your job progresses and you make more money, particularly if you resist lifestyle creep.

If you earn a substantial increase, take advantage of it by increasing your savings rate prior to actually purchasing a new car or planning a major getaway. Working to make sure your older self is very well cared for is another way to appreciate your achievements. Even though you get only a 3% expense boost, consider paying 2% into your retirement while keeping the other 1%.

Seek alternative strategies to redirect your spending to your retirement account. You could, for instance, settle off a vehicle and put the money into some IRA or contribute more to your employer's retirement plan. The above strategy works; since you seem to be paying a vehicle payment, allocating some towards your savings won't seem like you're biting from your discretionary spending.

Knowing the Ins and Outs of Retirement Accounts Is Essential

There seem to be contribution restrictions to contemplate with retirement accounts such as 401(k)s and IRAs. Although you may want to quickly boost your savings to catch up for the time you lost up to now, you can really only deposit so much money into such accounts. People below the age of 50 could contribute up to $19,500 to a 401(k) account and $6,000 to an IRA account in 2020 (DeMatteo, 2020).

Withdrawing money from a regular, or pre-tax, 401(k)

and/or IRA account prior to the age of 59 and a half carries a significant penalty. You could withdraw penalty-free the after-tax money you've put into a Roth 401(k) or Roth IRA before retirement, but you must wait until you're 59 and a half to do so. Several IRA accounts charge a premium if you make withdrawals before an account has been active for five years (DeMatteo, 2020).

Keeping this in mind, you must try to avoid taking money from such accounts. Even though you may be excited to start saving and investing, bear in mind that it's critical to have a robust emergency cushion and a real plan for debt repayment. All of these factors are critical when planning for a secure financial future.

Necessary Tips to Get You Started With Investing

There are a lot of ways to put your money to work for you. Options like stocks, bonds, ETFs, Index funds, and much more are available in the market for you to grow your wealth. However, the option you choose to put your money in should be based on your goals, either short-term or long-term.

Investing is not meant for only the super-wealthy Wall Street executives. As a matter of fact, one of the most prevailing methods for Americans to turn into billionaires is through investments in stock markets. Learning investing might seem daunting at first, but it is not quite as complex as it may seem.

Prior to investing, you should prepare yourself well

enough to deal with the outcomes. You must ensure the following factors:

1. Having a comfortable budget–earnings, spending, savings per month
2. Controlling debt–no more high-interest credit card balances
3. Realistic and precise goals–your vision must be clear for the future

You do not really have to wait until you get rid of your debts in order to start investing. If you want your earnings to rise significantly, you must invest. Even though holding funds in a savings account seems to be a secure bet, the interest you will generate is insufficient to match inflation over several years. Despite being highly risky in the short term, the stock exchange provides compounded gains that not only keep up with but surpass inflation over the long run.

Let's say you obtained a little fortune which you choose to invest. Now, if you took $5,000 and invested it in an account that offers a 7% interest rate while adding a few extra $200 per month for approximately 30 years–you are going to have somewhere around $284,000.

Other than traditional retirement accounts, investing in other options might seem intriguing to you. Why don't we give you a go-through of various options to invest in like stocks, ETFs, bonds, and more?

Mutual Funds

Almost similar to ETFs, mutual funds combine lots

and lots of separate stocks into a single investment. The only difference between these two involves how they are sold and priced. Prices of ETFs vary in real-time and you can trade them as frequently as you desire when the market is open. However, in the case of mutual funds, they entail restrictions on how often you may trade them while being priced only once per day.

Bonds

Owning separate bonds is indeed an efficient investment approach. A bond index fund will help you build bonds in your portfolio (could be a mutual fund or ETF). Should you participate in the diversified fund or a Robo-advisor, bond exposure would be included based on the product's objectives and risk management.

Real Estate

Let us clear you on one thing; real estate investment does not mean owning the house you live in. Investments in real estate mean owning commercial buildings or apartments and then leasing them. Even though the value of real estate appreciates over time, the power of investment is hidden in the form of cash received from tenants.

Owning real estate may provide revenue that you can keep in your pocket or reinvest if you could somehow charge greater rent than you splurge on for mortgages, maintenance, and taxes.

Understanding when and how to invest in property will be a significantly wider subject than we can discuss within this book. However, there are ways to engage quickly on a reasonable budget. Two real estate investing platforms that crowdsource investment opportunities are

"Fundraise" and "Roofstock," to name a few (Weliver, 2021a). You may spend as little as $5,000 and earn from massive office projects or apartments with other investors.

Such trades are not beyond risks, as well as the fees charged by the businesses reducing returns. They may, however, be appealing if you really desire to bring real estate exposure to your portfolio without having to take on the burden of managing and purchasing the estates by yourself.

Investments That Are Advanced

In recent times, brokerages increasingly removed trading costs as well as simplified the procedure to purchase minor stock shares. Previously, if a stock priced $500 per share, then one would need $500 to purchase a single share. You could as well be given a commission of $5 every time you buy or sell shares.

As for today, you have the freedom to invest with as little as a few bucks and not be charged any commission. If a person got $50, they could easily purchase one-tenth of a $500 stock share.

According to research, purchasing index funds and holding them for decades is the smartest way to invest. The very approach almost always outperforms even the most experienced Wall Street investors. Hence, dreadfully boring as well.

This is where we recommend you invest the majority of your earnings. Nevertheless, it is okay to allocate 10% or 5% of your income to "game" by performing relatively frequent transactions.

It encourages people to have fun while learning

through performing more frequent trading without risking your money. The brilliance of diversity is that you will always profit from any investment that does favorably, while several underperforming stocks will not bankrupt you. Should you make poor choices and choose your own stocks, you could end up losing the majority of your wealth.

Best Ways to Invest

Personal financial planning is just that: personal. The smartest possible road for one person to make investments will differ from the best way for someone else to make investments. Certain aspects, on the other hand, are generic. All of us need to put money aside for retirement that we will forget about for many years. We ought to think about our future selves, and saving sufficient income to survive well in retirement is a difficult challenge. The earlier you financialize, the smoother it should be.

• **Robo-Advisors**

Look for a Robo-advisor if you wish to keep things as simple as possible. By using tech means, these advisors invest your money in a very diversified and broad portfolio of bonds and stocks which are optimized as per your objectives and tolerance of risk. Moreover, the account opening procedure is also as simple as answering some 12-question quiz. Best part? Robo-advisers are very inexpensive and they do not even require you to maintain a minimum balance.

- **Stock Brokerage**

If you consider Robo-advisors to be some kind of restaurant serving you pre-prepared meals, then stock brokerage can be considered as the supermarket of investments. You can have anything you wish to have, but you must know how to prepare those things.

If you are a person who knows what they want and sees things from a certain perspective and further expects things to be exact, this is for you. However, if you are a person who neither knows what they want nor knows how to get it, this is not a good choice for you.

Well, with the help of a stock brokerage, anyone can create their own buy-and-hold portfolio by combining several exchange-traded funds. Again, you could also purchase individual stocks as frequently as you like.

Building Your Net Worth

Although the investment portfolio is indeed an important element of the net worth calculation, which can be easily calculated by summing the worth of assets and deducting debt value, this isn't going to be the only factor that might make significant contributions to your financial well-being in retirement. Here we have five strategies for boosting your net worth.

- **Purchase a Property**

Property indeed has the power to become your most valuable asset. A lot of folks sell their homes after retiring to survive old age. Real estate can prove to be a great asset since its value appreciates over time (as mentioned earlier). But since we witnessed the Great Recession, it is not guaranteed that the value will always appreciate.

Whereas leasing could be less expensive, allowing you to subsequently invest the difference to possibly gain so much over time rather than buying a home, property investment practically compels you to save. Your net will grow as you pay down your mortgage and the value of your home improves.

- **Trade a Business**

A business can significantly increase or decrease a person's net worth. Although several businesses offer a comfortable life for their proprietors, they are an asset that is difficult to appraise and sell, making it non-liquidating. However, valuing a business is more complicated than valuing a property; therefore, consult with a professional who really can assist you in establishing a valuation and determining the net worth of your business.

- **Increase Your Income**

Most individuals seek to accumulate progressively enormous sums of money over the course of their lives.

More money means more opportunities to pay off debt, save, invest in other assets, etc.

- **Pay Down the Debts**

Debt reduction improves overall net worth; therefore, do what you must to wipe off your auto loan, home, and credit card debt with time. Simultaneously, start by cutting down on a few of your expenditures. The fewer your expenditures, the more valued you are–plus, the more money you could save.

- **Life Insurance**

This might seem out of place to include here;, however, the net worth of your family would obviously collapse if you died suddenly and they were unable to make a livelihood. Think about buying life insurance to protect your family. This will not benefit you in retirement (although a few types may have an investing aspect which you can access later on down the line), but this will support your dependents if anything really turns out badly.

4

DOWNSIZING FOR RETIREMENT

*D*ownsizing is a great option for anyone seeking retirement. It has its pros and cons, but mostly it proves to be quite beneficial. Downsizing requires hard work, patience, and planning. It entails arranging your present residence, giving up on unnecessary stuff, listing your residence in the market to be sold, and eventually relocating to a new area.

Many people pay experts to help them through this phase, while others look upon their family or friends. A lot of senior Americans are now opting to live a modest retirement; 46% of baby boomers who sold their houses in the year 2017 were downsizing, according to a Zillow report (Christian, 2021).

Downsizing can be daunting, a big decision that is factored by emotional and financial circumstances. It is not easy to declutter a huge house. Leaving your home, seeking a new home, plus relocating your stuff can all bring a person to hardship. Throughout this chapter, we will delve through the factors of why folks downsize for retirement and offer tips from professionals about how to make the shift. We will also be considering other stages, including preparing your property for sale and evaluating relocation expenses.

Your Motives for Relocating

Shifting or relocating to a new area is quite stressful no matter what age you are. Even the young kids find it challenging when they are told that they will be changing their current residence. Likewise, retirement downsizing entails daunting challenges within itself as well.

However, determining your motives for downsizing will help you stay on track and feel less emotional about the materialistic stuff. According to a Merrill Lynch survey conducted in 2018, the top reason stated by participants for relocating in retirement was to live near family (Christian, 2021). The goal to minimize expenditures was a secondary concern.

Downsizing is not something that is chosen by everyone consciously. Because of progressively deteriorating health, the death of a spouse, or perhaps an unanticipated financial crisis, relocation could be both immediate and unavoidable. Recognize your personal motive for relocating. Analyze the benefits and drawbacks so you'll be confident in your choices.

These questions might prove to be advantageous for consideration:

- How much money plus time are you able to commit to a shift in your life?
- What kind of sacrifices are you truly up for?
- Where do you wish to live?
- Is living in the same area a better option or would you want new experiences?
- What kind of house would be easy to navigate?
- For comfort, how much space would you need?

One more thing which is necessary is to communicate and talk through with your family as early as possible. If you are married, talk through anything about which your significant other will have concerns.

Also, ensure that your children are always aware of what's happening or what is about to happen. Allow them to come over and help you with the packing if this is the house they grew up in. This is ultimately going to prevent any kind of resentment or conflict down the road.

Financial Consequences of Downsizing

Of course, to save those bucks, people downsize. Inexpensive housing and living expenditures are a great way to save those dollars for future purposes. There are many perks to downsizing, and you will be happy to downsize after knowing them.

- **Cash flow increases**

A windfall of cash results when you sell your home.

This eventually grows a retirement nest egg along with boosting your savings.

- **Mortgage reduction**

If you haven't paid off your present home's mortgage, the new property with reduced monthly payments of mortgage will be nice for your budget. Those few bucks that you would save each month could be used for a yearly venture in the Maldives or even to finance your grandchild's education.

- **Reduced utility bills**

Reduced utility expenditures are associated with smaller premises and fewer rooms. You might save even more money if you move to a property featuring new windows or energy-efficient appliances.

- **Lesser maintenance and cleaning**

Every year, Americans 50 years and older spend nearly $90 billion on home maintenance, accounting for 47% of the national total (Christian, 2021). A modern home would most likely require minimal fixes and also have cheaper maintenance expenditures than an older house. Plus, you won't be spending quite so many dollars employing someone to look after the house.

However, before you begin relocating, make sure you have a firm grasp of your finances. If you do not pay much attention or keep your eyes open, hidden charges and poor planning will most likely chip away potential savings. Leaving your current residence and moving to a newer one is never cheap.

Let's be honest, you end up spending more than you planned to when you relocate. This is exactly why we recommend you consult with moving companies and obtain estimates to plan your budget accordingly.

During major changes in our lives, we tend to believe, "Alright–I'm going through a major change so it is completely fine to spend more money than planned. I will cover it up later." You must not fall into this pit of eventual guilt which will eat you up. Instead, be smart in planning your budget and then stick to it.

Consider Expenses Before You Move

You need to know what expenses will occur when you relocate. As obvious, moving entails lots and lots of effort plus legal procedures and then mental stress, but you should also be aware of the incurring expenses in between and prior to it.

- **HAF–Homeowners Association Fees**

If you relocate to a townhouse, community, or neighborhood with a homeowner's association or HOA, you will be required to pay monthly fees. HOA fees differ wildly, although some estimates predict expenditures ranging from $100 to $700 a month. Fees are determined by the benefits rendered by the HOA; for example, lawn maintenance. The greater the HOA costs, the more services and perks there are.

- **Preparing Your Home for Market**

The process of preparing your property for sale in the property market is known as staging. This could involve a variety of activities, such as repainting the walls and replacing old flooring with new ones, or landscape upgrades and changing bathroom faucets. These are not inexpensive, but might be required if you do not wish for your house to remain in the market for an indefinite period of time. Include important home maintenance on your list as well.

- **Homeowner Property and Insurance Tax**

Moving to a smaller place does not mean that you are no longer required to pay insurance tax. The locality where you are moving to really matters. There could be external factors such as proximity to natural hazards or even crime rates which can increase premiums of insurance. To seek the optimal price, check prices on the very same policy from multiple insurance companies. Keep an eye out for alterations to your property tax bill as well.

- **Estate Agent Charges**

A real estate agent's usual commission is roughly 6%

of the home's sale price. If you are selling a $250,000 property, the purchasing and selling agents might each collect $15,000 in commission. Now that's a lot of cash. The words of wisdom? Closure fees and agency charges will reduce your ultimate payment.

- **Shopping Spree for New Home**

While you downsize and try to cut expenses, you may add more to the shopping spree for your new home. We tend to buy a lot of things from Target and Home Depot when we are on the move (which we do not necessarily need). We recommend that you be careful while buying things for your new home and save up for your future.

Let the Downsizing Begin

You have finally made the decision to downsize and move. It is time to start collecting your possessions and putting them in a box. But where do you start? It's not a simple procedure, of course, but people have made their careers out of helping others downsize for retirement, so it makes sense.

It might feel challenging, but do not let the daunting experience overwhelm you at all. The confusion between what to keep and what to give away may drive you crazy. In fact, it is one of the reasons why people are afraid, to begin with. You must establish goals and objectives and also set timelines for them. Hold yourself accountable for what matters.

If you prepare yourself for where you are headed and what you are going to achieve, it will get less challenging. Once a person starts visualizing their end goal and knows exactly what the outcomes are going to be, it becomes smooth.

One Step at a Time

Rushing things can escalate and turn out to be more stressful than they already are. Take baby steps first. Start with the smallest room, the smallest space. Tackle one thing at a time and do not over-pressure yourself into thinking you need to do it quickly.

The process of downsizing usually takes months to complete. It cannot be done simply over a weekend, like throwing a party. It takes a lot of time to pack up, move, and settle. It would be great if you laid down a proper plan for your downsizing. Listing down every priority as per your need and checking it every day can help you remember so many things.

Be Realistic, and Be Rational

It is very common to fall in love with your stuff. And letting things go could trigger a lot of emotions and memories. Downsizing entails leaving 70 to 80% of the stuff which took you around 20 to 30 years to stock up (Christian, 2021). Be realistic and start acting rationally. Do not look at things with emotions and longing. Look at the things with the perspective of them being used within a year. If you find something that you won't be needing for another couple of years, let it go.

Make a habit of looking for apparent items you can get

rid of, such as identical home goods, obsolete papers, out-of-date apparel, and old newspapers.

Take Photos of Your Current Environment

If you know how your home always looks or how things are kept a certain way, it will be much easier for you to set your new home up. Document your rooms and keep them with you so you can see later what progress you have made; this can be quite comforting.

Check and write down the measurements of the furniture you intend to bring to verify it will fit in your new home. Document the placement of family photographs on the walls and the layout of furnishings. These will come in handy when you are unpacking at your new house.

Give Away Stuff You Do not Need Anymore

Marketing unneeded stuff is an excellent strategy to increase your moving funds. It moreover assists in clearing space, and there's a sense of accomplishment in understanding that your old stuff will help others. You may offer your items on websites such as Facebook Marketplace or Craigslist. Apps such as LetGo, OfferUp, and Next-Door.com are additional options. To prevent scammers, ensure only to accept cash proposals. For such interactions, you should hope to meet folks in a public venue.

Consider organizing a garage sale for minor or less valuable goods. Selling to hobbyists, used bookshops, music stores, or online auction sites are also choices. Return valuables to their rightful owners. You may still have your 40-year-old daughter's graduation gown stored in the closet. Ask directly if she still wants to keep it. Get rid of it if she doesn't.

Seek Professional Help

A whopping majority of enthusiasts offer their services to help retirees in downsizing. There are Senior Move Managers who specialize in assisting seniors along with their families to cope with the physical and emotional elements of relocating. Decluttering your house, having emotional support, facilitation of disposal, sale of undesired goods, donation, or even setting up processes can be done with the help of professional organizers.

These experts work for you. However, they do not offer cleaning services. Senior move managers are experts in assisting seniors and their families with the emotional and physical elements of relocating or aging in place. Professional organizers, on the other hand, can assist you with decluttering your house, providing emotional support, facilitating the disposal, donation, or sale of undesirable goods, and setting up processes to help you stay organized.

Rates may differ by state and employment, although they typically range from $75 to $150 per hour. Although this may appear to be an expensive option, the time and work you will save may be well worth it.

It is similar to hiring a wedding planner for a big wedding. Of course, you could do the work by yourself, but having professional help can do it seamlessly and with less stress. Such professionals frequently provide a range of activities that may be customized to match your budget. This isn't an exclusive distinctive luxury that only the wealthy can afford. Occasionally, people will only engage someone for a portion of the procedure.

Deal With Emotions

It's intimidating—and exhausting—to sift through a lifetime's worth of memories. Downsizing may bring up a plethora of feelings such as despair, worry, tension, and loss. Knowing the causes for these thoughts and employing ways to manage them might not always change how you feel, but might help the downsizing experience go much easier so that you can concentrate on your next phase, according to a 2018 letter from Harvard Medical School (Christian, 2021).

If an emotional turmoil gets to you, look for a friend or relative to talk to. Nearest and dearest people have the power to hear you reflect about precious items while gently nudging you to let go of stuff you no longer require. Our possessions have a habit of becoming like members of the household. Perhaps calling an old acquaintance after a tough day of tidying might help to soothe your emotions and help you stay focused. Consider seeking professional assistance if you do not have somebody to depend on. You might wish to chat with a therapist or see your healthcare physician.

Retirement Living: Renting Vs. Ownership

There may be compelling reasons to purchase a property in retirement, even though there are equally compelling ones to rent. If you do not have to pay for upkeep and repairs, the latter may be less expensive. Conversely, if you do not have to fear your landlord increasing your rent, homeownership would be less troublesome.

Accommodation expenditures will be one of your primary monthly expenses in retirement, regardless of whichever path you take. Here are a few things to think about while deciding whether to rent or purchase.

- **Risk**

In essence, purchasing a home after retiring is a better investment than renting. Owning a house, on the other hand, implies considerable financial risks. Expenses might rise above and beyond those of renting due to market swings, unforeseen maintenance bills, and insurance premiums. Plus, regardless of which choice you choose, keep in mind that taxes, rent, and insurance prices all rise with time.

However, one significant concern is the risk of upkeep that comes with homeownership. Renting is similar to purchasing a maintenance insurance policy; tenants are not responsible for routine maintenance bills, equipment breakdowns, or natural disasters such as flooding or storms.

- **Tax Implications**

Another key consideration when weighing the benefits of buying vs. renting is the tax consequences. Interest on eligible mortgages of $750,000 or less is deductible for a married couple filing jointly beginning with returns filed in 2019 (Probasco, 2021). Under the old legislation, you could still deduct interest on a $1 million or less mortgage if you acquired your property before Dec. 16, 2017 (Probasco, 2021).

Nevertheless, because property tax deductions, which were once a huge benefit to tax-paying citizens (particularly in wealthy neighborhoods), have now been capped at $10,000 and the standard deduction has nearly doubled, thanks to the Tax Cuts and Jobs Act of 2017, the number of people who will itemize their deductions to save money has decreased significantly. Since rental prices are not tax deductible, renters are unable to take advantage of these potential savings (Probasco, 2021).

- **Liquidity and Cashing Out**

The independence from stressing about home market circumstances and liquidity is another financial benefit of being a renter. Selling a house takes time, involves a great deal of documentation, and most realtors charge a fee, reducing the investment returns. Whenever it's necessary to relocate, dodging these snares may be well worth the hassle.

Many retirees rely primarily on pension plans, whether through social security, government or union plans, or an annuity. People often do not have access to significant amounts of cash on hand. The normal expenditures of owning a house might be disastrous if you do not have enough assets on hand to cover unforeseen needs.

- **Opportunity of Investment (Is It Really?)**

Even while real estate could be an excellent investment, a property must not be acquired just for that purpose. Accommodation is an inherent expense of life, and selling an investment item must not require you to relocate. Once it comes to housing expenditures, retirees just shouldn't consider the investment opportunities of owning a home.

For utilizing property as an investment, a landowner would need to purchase low and sell high—opportunistically purchasing and selling residences. Conversely, by selling a property for a profit at a time while prices are rising, one risks being priced out of the market if values keep rising. Anyone on a fixed income, such as most retirees, might not even be able to acquire these items.

Renting is similar to shorting a stock in terms of economics. One may rent an apartment, waiting for those prices to fall, and afterward purchase a property later if they feel housing prices are heading down. Being inaccurate regarding the actual trend of property prices and having to offer a hefty purchase amount to cover a short position is analogous to being incorrect about the future of stock markets and having to offer a hefty purchasing price to cover a short position.

Benefits of Homeownership

The fact that you do not have a mortgage payment

does not really make this an easy decision. Property taxes and maintenance expenditures must be considered, and the older your property is, the greater the cost your repairs may be. Even yet, it's simple to come up with reasons to stay—especially if you already own your home (and have no medical misfortune to leave). Here are a few more crucial points to consider.

- Equity
- Tax Deductions
- Stableness

Benefits of Renting

There are advantages to selling your property and shifting into a rental. These advantages are familiar to those who now rent. Whether you are an independent adult looking to downsize or aren't certain where you will devote your retirement, renting can be a good option. For a few years, you could wish to relocate for better weather or a reduced cost of living, but you will be able to simply return to your family afterward.

However, unless you are a homeowner thinking about selling, below are some things to think about.

- Little to no maintenance or responsibility
- Moving flexibility
- Liquidity
- Fewer taxes and costs

The question of whether to maintain the ancestral

mansion or move to a smaller house is a challenging thing for a lot of individuals close to retirement. If you really do opt to relocate, you will have to deal with the worry and expenditure that comes with owning a property. When deciding whether to buy or rent a property in retirement, there are various factors to consider, including:

- What would be the tax advantages of renting versus buying?
- Is your house a possible investment or simply another added cost?
- Which dangers, in regards to unforeseen expenditures, occur with ownership, and would your budget handle them?

Considering these, we presume it will get a lot easier for you to decide whether to downsize or stay where you prefer to live.

Mistakes People Make While Downsizing

Often folks fantasize of funding a significant portion of their retirement by selling their existing house, purchasing a smaller property, and investing the difference for income. In actuality, though, they frequently make significantly less money than they had imagined.

Downsizing can still be a beneficial decision if done correctly. You may not only walk out the door with more money, but also with a simpler life and lower home-maintenance and utility expenses for years to come. To achieve that pleasant ending, you must avoid the unanticipated hazards that make downsizing so risky. Below are a few mistakes and traps that await downsizers.

- **Overestimating the Value of Your Current Residence**

It's tempting to daydream about how much money your property will bring in. Maybe the neighbors down the block decided to sell for a hefty price and were last seen loading their new Bentley and traveling to Mexico. You likely wouldn't understand three essential things: how much they really made from the transaction, how their home varies from yours in terms of the traits that prospective buyers most value, and if the real estate market was better or worse at the time.

Try consulting many local real estate agents for an unbiased evaluation of your home's actual market valuation. Acquiring more than one is vital, since an agent who really is desperate for your listing may offer you an overly optimistic estimate. You might also employ a third-party appraiser.

- **Underestimating the Cost of Purchasing a New Home**

Folks are inclined to believe that they will get a good deal on the next property they purchase, exactly as they are likely to believe that they will get a good deal on their existing property. It's important to keep in mind that the prospective investors of your present home—as well as the sellers of your future one—are thinking along the same lines.

Use multiple resources to examine previous sales prices to determine what you may expect to spend for the sort of property you want to buy. If you're considering relocating to a new place, there's no alternative for spending time there and looking at suitable properties. Even if you're familiar with a location from previous vacations, it may be worthwhile to visit at different times of the year to ensure that you'll be pleased there all year long.

- **Ignoring the Tax Consequences**

Except if you earn a huge profit on the sale of your property (and if you do, congrats), you may not have to pay any income tax on the profit. Current IRS regulations enable most couples to deduct up to $500,000 in capital gains from their taxable income. In most cases, singles can exclude up to $250,000. The guidelines also consider how long you've owned and lived in the house, among other things (Daugherty, 2021).

Regardless of not owing income tax, there are indeed tax factors to consider before relocating. Property taxes are high in several popular retirement areas. A low-tax area may have higher sales or income taxes, or it may tax your pension income differently.

- **Forgetting to Consider Closing Costs**

If you haven't bought a house in years, you might well have started to forget about the closing fees you will have to pay at the moment. These were most likely legal expenses, service charges, title insurance, and a slew of other things. When you buy your next house, you will not only have to pay closing costs, but you will also have to pay a second set as a home seller.

Agent charges are adjustable, so aim to secure the most beneficial, feasible amount from the start. As a purchaser, you may be able to persuade an enthusiastic seller to cover part of the closing expenses, but keep in mind that whoever buys your property will almost certainly try the same trick on you.

Although downsizing your house might help you save money for retirement, you should do your homework beforehand. You could discover ways to save money on the transfer that you weren't aware of, or you might decide it's better to stay there for the time being.

5

HEALTH AND MEDICAL PLANNING

$\mathcal{A}$ mong the most significant expenses during retirement is healthcare. In 2020, a 65-year-old couple retiring in 2020 may expect to spend $295,000 on healthcare and medical bills. This does not include the extra yearly cost of long-term care, which, according to long-term care insurance Genworth, was $105,852 in 2020 for a private room in a nursing facility (Lake, 2021b).

Many retirees aren't emotionally or financially prepared for the hefty costly medical expenditures of retirement, despite saving and planning for it their whole working life. Whether you are just starting out in your career, nearing retirement, or making the transition out of the workforce, it is critical to plan for your medical insurance and to be on the safe side.

The amount of money flowing in each month, as well as the total cost of your spending, will determine your ultimate retirement budgeting. Only 51% of persons aged 60 and over think they are on pace to meet their retirement goals. The average monthly expenditure for persons aged 65 and over is $4,238. Nevertheless, for individuals who retire at full retirement age in 2021, social security will only pay a maximum monthly payment of $3,148; the maximum amount will increase to $3,345 in 2022 (Lake, 2021b).

It is indeed crucial to note that social security is only intended to supplement retirement money: according to the Social Security Administration (SSA), social security replaces 40% of pre-retirement income on average. Annual cost-of-living adjustments (COLAs)—increases to keep up with inflation—affect benefits as well (Lake, 2021b).

However, the issue remains that, in order to meet medical expenses, you will most likely need to search outside of social security. The amount of retirement funds you should set up for healthcare is mostly determined by your age and general well-being. The healthier we are as we approach retirement, the less income we would have to spend on medical expenses. On the other hand, a healthy lifestyle leads to a higher life expectancy, thus retirees should budget for a longer retirement period.

Well-being expenditures can easily consume a large portion of a retirement plan. Calculating such expenditures and devising a spending strategy might help you save far more of your retirement funds for other purposes.

Going Beyond Retirement Savings

Increasing healthcare expenditures shouldn't have to deplete your savings. Pre-retirees do have the option to set up a healthcare safety net in two directions.

- Long-Term Care Insurance
- Health Savings Account (HSA)

Long-Term Care Insurance

This sort of coverage can provide a monthly benefit towards long-term care over a certain period of time (generally around two to five years) or even for the rest of your life. Premiums for long-term care insurance might not have been affordable for everybody. Purchasing a life insurance policy with the possibility of adding a long-term care insurance rider is yet another possibility. This helps younger individuals to have a strong foothold on long-term care planning, since the earlier one purchases life or long-term care insurance, the cheaper the rates are expected to be.

Health Savings Account

HSAs (Health Savings Accounts) are a fantastic method to save enough for medical expenses in retiring years. This solution, however, is just not accessible to everybody and also has limitations. HSAs are only accessible to individuals who have high-deductible health insurance policies and no other coverage. As of 2019, an insurance policy must have a deductible of at least $1,350 for self-only coverage and $2,700 for family coverage to be called a high-deductible plan (Silvestrini, 2021b). Preventative care services are not subjected to these deductibles.

Eligible people for Medicare or who are reported as dependents on someone else's taxes are not eligible for HSA accounts. Pre-tax deposits are made into the accounts to meet healthcare expenditures which are not covered by insurance. Unused funds in an HSA are carried forward year after year. The accounts are also transferable, meaning they follow you along whether you move jobs or retire.

According to Healthcare.gov, if you have a high-deductible health plan, you can contribute up to $3,500 for self-only coverage and up to $7,000 for family coverage to an HSA in 2019. You can contribute up to $3,550 for single coverage and $7,100 for family coverage in 2020. According to the Internal Revenue Service, if you are 55 at the end of the tax year, you can contribute an extra $1,000 to your HAS (Silvestrini, 2021b).

People who do have HSAs, and those who are qualified but still haven't created one, are actually losing out on a brilliant way to save for retirement. It's time for a new fad to emerge.

Using HSAs

Withdrawals from an HSA to pay for eligible medical costs are tax-free. This offers investors a significant benefit over IRAs and 401(k)s, which require payouts to be taxed. You would pay a 20% tax penalty if you are under the age of 65 and use the cash for other reasons. Withdrawals for other uses, meanwhile, are taxed just like withdrawals from those other qualifying retirement savings accounts, e.g., 401(k)s, if you are above 65.

Dental treatment and hearing aids are examples of qualified health costs that are not covered under the Medicare Part. Certain Medicare Advantage Plans provide additional benefits not available via Original Medicare, including vision, dental care, and hearing. HSA money could also be utilized to pay for particular health insurance premiums, such as the following:

- Continued healthcare coverage (such as COBRA)
- By obtaining unemployment compensation, you can get health insurance
- Long-term Care Insurance
- If you are older than 65 years, you may well be eligible for Medicare and other health insurance (with the exception of Medicare supplemental policies, such as Medigap)

Tax efficiency and HSAs go along quite well. There are numerous ways to make HSAs work for you even if you are still working, getting prepared to retire, or have Medicare on retirement. Take into consideration the following ways you can benefit from HSAs:

Get to Know the Triple Tax Advantage

The majority of Americans think of HSAs as a method to save enough for current health bills that aren't covered by insurance. However, if you really can cover these expenditures out of pocket, an HSA could be a strong driver for retirement funds owing to its triple tax-free status.

Often people contribute to HSAs pre-tax via payroll taxes at the job, allowing them to avoid FICA taxes on healthcare payments. You can benefit from HSA outside of your employment as well by using after-tax money, subsequently deducting from their own taxes.

An HSA can also be acquired outside of the workplace and funded using after-tax money, which the individual can subsequently deduct from their own taxes. These contributions are tax-deductible and could be used to compensate for present and future eligible health expenses, even those in retirement.

Since HSAs are considered to be one of the most tax-free and effective savings alternatives, current healthcare bills can be paid with other personal assets by contributing in full.

Do not use an HSA if it is not required essentially, making it truly beneficial and compounding to work for you. For long-term growth potential, consider putting a part of your HSA in a non-cash investment option. Consider how HSAs can help you save money on taxes: When do you want to pay taxes upon HSA profits and contributions? Today? Afterward? What if I said never? (If you are using it to pay for healthcare expenditures that qualify). Sure, anyone may use their Roth IRA to pay for medical bills, but you have already paid the tax.

Set Aside Money Just for Healthcare

You have probably put money aside in a 529 college

savings account for your kid's future. It's a type of account that allows you to set aside money for a certain cost in the future. Much of your money might be set aside for specific financial objectives including a new vehicle, a memorable holiday package, or a bigger house. The investing aim does have a varied timeframe in each scenario and therefore should be approached differently.

Consider healthcare costs. You will almost certainly have to pay for medical operations, medical fees, prescription medications, and possibly even home care or nursing home care in the future. Nobody guarantees when these expenditures arise or even how much you will be required to pay.

Building a nest egg expressly geared to assist and cover future healthcare expenditures is a wise choice because you will almost certainly have to pay for sizable healthcare bills later on in life. But just how much money should you put aside?

According to the Fidelity Retiree Health Care Cost Estimate, in 2021, an average retired couple age 65 will require nearly $300,000 in after-tax savings to pay healthcare bills (Fidelity, 2021).

Even though you may not have an HSA, it is a good idea to set away some assets solely for medical costs. One of your top five costs in retirement will almost certainly be healthcare.

Hence, to help pay for expected medical expenditures, consider earmarking a portion of your 401(k)s or IRAs (together with their possible future gains).

Put Your HSA Money to Good Use by Investing It

Despite wellness expenses that keep on growing, there really are steps you can do now to prepare for a flood of healthcare expenses when you retire. However, you must begin saving immediately and put those funds to work through investing.

Set aside some of your HSA in cash to pay immediate medical bills, and invest the remainder for possible tax-free appreciation as well as to support your savings for retirement.

You may have a high enough account balance to begin investing in mutual funds, stocks, or bonds if you have established a cash buffer in your HSA to cover short-term, unplanned, and eligible medical expenditures and out-of-pocket maximum deductible restrictions.

All You Need to Know About Medicare

To make you feel comfortable and confident about enrolling in Medicare, we will answer some key questions that you may have. But do keep in mind that changes have been made to Medicare coverage by the Federal Government in accordance with the 2020 pandemic.

What Is Medicare?

The official government institutions in charge of Medicare are the Centers for Medicare and Medicaid Services. Medicare is a government health insurance program that covers certain young people with any disabilities, people aged 65 or above, and people who have End Stage Renal Disease (ESRD). This is a condition where the kidneys are in permanent failure and require constant dialysis or a kidney transplant.

Some would be surprised to learn that Medicare only supports individuals. There is no family coverage policy under Medicare, unlike health insurance policies until age 65. This implies your spouse or children won't be accepted under your Medicare plan; they'll need to sign up for Medicare through their own means whenever they're ready.

You have seven months to join up/enroll with Medicare. For people who become eligible when they turn 65, the 7-month period begins three months before and ends three months after they turn 65 (Fidelity, 2021a). This is the time when you can enroll for the first time.

For individuals over 65 who are still employed and possess health insurance via their employment or spouse's employment, Medicare offers a Special Enrollment Period. You can also use this window if specific life circumstances occur, such as relocating or dropping another health insurance.

You could have a huge disparity in your medical insurance if you pass the Early Enrollment Period and do not fit again for the Special Enrollment Period. You will eventually end up waiting until the General Enrollment Period resumes in January the following year. (It'll be over in March.)

However, this is how skipping the Early Enrollment Period might cost you: If you enroll between January and March, the coverage won't begin till July of the upcoming year, and you would possibly be charged with a late enrollment penalty, which will be added to your monthly charge.

What Options Does Medicare Offer?

Choosing health insurance coverage while employed at past companies was quite simple prior to Medicare. You could choose a sole plan which would cover every medication, doctor's appointment, or medical requirement. On the other hand, Medicare is quite a unique plan made up of several components. Each component deals with a separate subject. To make things even more confusing, each section has a variety of alternatives inside it. Let's have a look at what we've got.

Part A – Hospital Insurance

Part A of Medicare was initially developed in 1965 to assist seniors in managing the high expense of hospitalization (Fidelity, 2021a). Hospital visits, specific medical treatments and operations, skilled nursing facility care, and hospice care are all covered in Part A.

Part B – Medical Insurance

Part B of Medicare pays for doctors' appointments and services, outpatient hospital care, lab testing, blood transfusions, physical and speech therapy, medical supplies and equipment, and emergency services, among other things. Original Medicare refers to both Part A and Part B taken together.

Medicare Supplement – Medigap

Medigap is a kind of private health insurance that ultimately compliments Medicare. This implies that it supports paying for part of the healthcare expenditures not being covered by the Original Medicare. Those leftover expenditures are referred to as the Medicare coverage "gaps."

Medicare will pay its part of covered healthcare expenditures if you have both Original Medicare plus Medigap coverage. Then your Medigap policy heads in and pays its share.

Parts A and B are provided by the federal government, whereas Medigap policies are provided by commercial health insurance firms. There are many Medigap plans to select from, all of which cover treatments not covered by Parts A and B.

Prescription Drug Coverage

Prescription drugs are not covered in the Original Medicare and Medigap plans. Therefore, you will need to buy the Part D plan or a Medicare advantage policy that does it. However, if you do not sign up for a Part D plan when you first become eligible, you may face financial penalties if you do so later. It's crucial to think about which prescription drug plans cover the prescriptions you need, where you buy them, and how often you need them, regardless of which plan you pick.

Medicare Advantage

Part A, Part B, and Medigap are not covered with this plan. Medicare Advantage (commonly known as Medicare Part C) is an all-around healthcare insurance plan that includes Original Medicare and Medigap coverage, as well as Part D prescription drug coverage, dental care, and vision treatments.

Isn't it fantastic? There is, however, a catch. "In-network services" are covered under Medicare Advantage plans. Every Medicare Advantage plan collaborates with a community of doctors and other healthcare providers. Often these Medicare Advantage plans compel beneficiaries to seek treatments within their community, but policies differ.

Consider the doctors you already visit, your present healthcare requirements (such as prescription drugs), and if the doctors you currently see will be in for the Medicare plan you are seeking while shopping for a Medicare Advantage plan. Will you bother changing physicians if they're not in-network?

Choosing the Right Plan for You

To determine which Medicare plan is the best possible one for you, it will always be a good place to begin by reviewing the insurance you currently have from your current healthcare provider. What might you maintain and what would you end up changing? Simplify your possibilities by asking yourself the following questions:

1. What advantages do I require? (You might just save dollars if you do not purchase insurance for benefits that you are willing to pay for out of pocket.)
2. Would I like to be able to pick my own physicians and healthcare providers?
3. How much money is affordable for you to spend on insurance (premiums) and healthcare?
4. What are the costs of each plan in comparison to other plans with similar benefits?

5. Is there coverage for my specific scenario in the plan? (If you plan to travel, paying for emergencies outside your state or nation may be necessary.)

The local SHIP office should assist you in comparing Medigap and Medicare Advantage plan benefits and pricing in your state.

Never Overlook the Cost of Healthcare

When estimating their retirement expenditures, many retirees and folks about to move out of the workforce neglect to include healthcare. Why is this? The major part of the cost (typically about 75%) is covered by their employer, while the residual cost (probably over 20-30%) is deducted from their salary. They believe they require the very same sum of take-home income as they do today; however, they overlook the fact that they would be liable for health insurance premiums on top of out-of-pocket expenses.

You will pay the usual premium amount plus an Income Related Monthly Adjustment Level if your modified adjusted gross income (MAGI) as recorded on your IRS tax return from two years ago is over a specific portion (IRMAA). IRMAA seems to be a charge that is applied to your insurance premium (Anspach, 2021).

Worst-Case Scenario

Total premiums and out-of-pocket payments for a 65-year-old guy were predicted to be around $4,500 per year by a calculator. That indicates if you haven't budgeted $375 a month for healthcare expenses, you will be tight on money. It was also anticipated that such healthcare expenditures will climb at nearly double the rate of inflation, which implies that $375 a month in retirement might be closer to $675 a month 10 years later (using a 6% inflation rate) (Anspach, 2021). You will need to multiply those figures by two for a married pair. Painful.

6

INSURANCE AND COVER FOR RETIREMENT

*T*his globe can be a dangerous and unpredictable place. People can be affected by a variety of disasters, and we as a species have survived owing to shared experience and capabilities by all, and the technological explosion of the last century is based on cumulative efforts. A wonderful idea would be a technique for mitigating risk in a pool, dispersing the risk across members so that no single party is left to bear the load alone. The mechanism in question is insurance.

Insurance is a system in which the insurer promises to compensate the insured or provide services to the insured in the case of certain unexpected events resulting in losses over a period of time in exchange for a fee that is normally agreed upon in advance. As a result, it is a strategy for dealing with risk. Its main purpose is to replace ambiguity with certainty in terms of the economic cost of loss-producing occurrences (Greene, 2021).

Insurance entails collecting funds from a number of insured businesses (referred to as exposures) to cover losses suffered by a few. The insured businesses are thus shielded against risk in exchange for a cost, which is determined by the severity and frequency of the incident. The risk insured against must have specific qualities in order to be insurable. Insurance is just a financial intermediary and is indeed a thriving industry and a significant element of the finance sector, but individuals and businesses can also self-insure by putting money aside to cover any unforeseeable consequences in the future.

Insurance may have a variety of social consequences depending on who faces the expense of damages and losses. So it has the potential to promote fraud; on the other hand, it has the potential to assist communities and people in preparing for disasters and mitigating the consequences of disasters on both families and society.

Insurance fraud, moral hazards, and preventative measures taken by the insurance firm can all impact the likelihood of losses. Moral hazard is a term used by insurance researchers to describe the higher risk caused by unintentional negligence, whereas insurance fraud is a term used to describe the increased risk caused by purposeful recklessness or disregard.

So much of the nerdy information you have taken in just by reading through these paragraphs is not to make the subject any more boring; let's jump right into the matter and see how insurance can be proven to be advantageous in your retirement.

Is Life Insurance a Necessity?

You have undoubtedly held life insurance for most of your adulthood. You might not have given it a second thought if your company included it in your salary and benefits. You were aware that it existed, although you didn't understand much about it. Alternatively, if you are a parent, you may very well have taken out a plan as part of smart budgeting.

However, currently you are on your way to the nest egg—or perhaps you have already retired. Your work no longer pays for life insurance, so you must determine whether to get a policy change or go into your golden years alone. What would be the best option?

Aren't you sick of hearing that there isn't a simple solution? This is due to the fact that your financial and investment accounts, as well as your needs, are distinct from those of your colleagues or relatives. What is really acceptable to someone might not be satisfactory to you.

What Role Does Life Insurance Play?

Most of the families utilize almost all of their income on lifestyle and its maintenance before retiring. When a couple of individuals work, both earnings are usually required to keep the family's quality of life afloat. The same would be applicable if only one person was working. When one of those income sources expires, the family may find itself in financial distress in the most inconvenient of situations.

The purpose of insurance coverage is to safeguard your household from losing money if you or another main income earner dies suddenly. Like every other thing, insurance also entails multiple types within itself.

Permanent life insurance, often known as cash-value insurance, is a type of life insurance that is frequently used in estate planning. It's available in two varieties: universal life and whole life. Term life insurance covers you for a specific amount of time, usually 10 to 30 years. The following are some considerations that may assist you in determining what you require.

- **Additional Sources of Income**

With the core purpose of insurance coverage, one could have a fair concept of their need for continued protection. In perhaps the simplest level, you probably do not need it if you've retired and aren't working to make a decent living. There are really no earnings to substitute if you're surviving off of social security and your retirement funds.

After you pass away, your family will keep receiving payments from your retirement funds, as well as a survivor benefit from social security. Nevertheless, your survivor benefit will vary depending on your specific circumstances, and it will be less than what social security provided when you were living. Before you get life insurance, be sure you understand your benefit.

- **Debts**

In an ideal world, you'll be debt-free when you retire,

but this isn't always the reality. In reality, according to 2018 research, 46 percent of homeowners aged 65 and over still had a mortgage, with 32 percent of those aged 70 and up still making payments in 2019. Student loan debt is expected to become more of a concern for retirees in the future. Senior citizens' school loan debt has climbed by 71.5 percent in the last five years, either because of leftover debts or because of co-signing loans for children or grandkids (Parker, 2021).

If you're still indebted, experts believe it's a good idea to keep your life insurance policy active. Unless the debt payments are such a small proportion of your total wealth that there is no possibility of financial hardship, choose the "better safe than sorry" strategy (Parker, 2021).

- **Is the Family Self-Sufficient?**

If your offspring have left the nest and are establishing their own households, plus your spouse is financially secure, you likely won't need insurance coverage. But on the other hand, if you have disabled children or children who are still living at home, you may prefer to retain it. In addition, if your spouse is to lose a significant portion of your pension benefits and perhaps other monthly income, life insurance might serve as a replacement for that void.

- **Is It Beneficial for Your Estate?**

Several folks with a lot of money might benefit from

life insurance in a strategic way, such as to cover inheritance taxes. It might be used to pay off corporate debt, estate buy-sell agreements, fund business, or even fund retirement plans.

As you might expect, determining how to employ life insurance as a tax-efficient aspect of your estate plan is a difficult task. You would need the assistance of an estate planning attorney. Take into account that estate tax issues are unlikely to apply unless your estate has a net value in the thousands of dollars. As a result, you might not even require life insurance for this reason, although you should see an expert to be sure.

This might seem counterintuitive to forego life insurance after such a long time; however, the fact is that you would no longer require it. If you have no income to substitute, almost no debt, a self-sufficient household, and no expensive worries about settling your property, you may be able to cancel that coverage. In terms of estate planning, you may require a different type of policy or significant revisions to your present one.

That would be an excellent issue for a service charge financial adviser or insurance advisor to answer. Be wary of merely asking your insurance representative for advice. Since they are frequently paid on commission, they may have an incentive to keep you on the insurance even if you do not need it.

Types of Life Insurance
There are several different forms of life insurance to suit a variety of requirements plus tastes. The key decision of whether to get temporary or permanent life insurance

is essential to consider based on the insured's short- or long-term needs.

Term Life Insurance

Term life insurance stretches for a specified term before expiring. When you buy insurance, you get to select the term. The most commonly used terms are 10, 20, and 30 years. The finest term life insurance plans strike a compromise between cost and long-term financial viability.

- A type of renewable term life insurance in which the coverage decreases at a specified rate over the policy's life is the **Decreasing Term Life Insurance.**
- Allowing policyholders to change a term policy to permanent insurance is the **Convertible Term Life Insurance.**
- Providing a quote for the year the policy is bought is **Renewable Term Life Insurance.** Increasing premiums annually, this type is generally the least expensive in the beginning.

Permanent Life Insurance

Only if the policyholder refuses to pay premiums or backs down from the policy, permanent life insurance remains in effect for the rest of the insured's life. It is usually more costly than a term loan. This type entails other kinds within itself as discussed below:

- **Whole Life:** This is the type of insurance that

accumulates cash with time. Allowing the policyholder to utilize the cash as per his/her needs, this could prove to be beneficial.

- **Universal Life:** Universal life is a form of permanent life insurance with a cash value feature that produces interest and variable premiums. Apart from term and whole life insurance, premiums can be changed over the years and the life insurance can be set at a fixed amount or increase over time.

- **Indexed Universal:** The cash value component of this form of universal life insurance allows the insured to receive a set or equity-indexed rate of return.

- **Variable Universal:** The policyholder can invest the cash worth of his or her variable universal life insurance policy in a different account if one is available. It also offers adjustable premiums and may be customized to provide a fixed or growing death benefit.

Final cost insurance, also known as burial insurance, is a form of permanent life insurance with a low death value. Beneficiaries can utilize the death benefit in whatever way they like, regardless of the names.

Term Vs. Permanent Life Insurance

In various aspects, term life insurance distinguishes itself from permanent life insurance, yet it tends to suit the needs of the majority of individuals. Term life insurance is only good for a fixed length of time and pays out a death benefit if the insured dies just before the term expires.

As long as the insured pays the premiums, permanent life insurance is in force. Another significant distinction is premiums: term life is often significantly less expensive than permanent life since it does not need the accumulation of financial value.

Do not apply for life insurance unless you assess your financial position and estimate how much income is needed to sustain your dependents' level of living or to satisfy the requirement for which you're acquiring a policy.

If you are the primary caregiver for children aged two and four, for instance, you will need adequate insurance to meet your custodial duties until your children are old enough to sustain themselves. You could figure out how much it would cost to employ a housekeeper and a nanny vs. using professional childcare and a cleaning company, and afterward add some cash for schooling.

In your life insurance estimate, factor in any outstanding mortgages and retirement expenses for your spouse. Particularly if one of the spouses has a lower income or is an unemployed parent. If you can handle it, sum up these fees over the next 16 or so years, plus inflation, and that is the insurance premium you might wish to buy.

How Much Life Insurance Should You Purchase?

The expense of life insurance premiums is influenced by a variety of factors. Sometimes factors seem beyond your disposal, but you can always regulate other parameters to cut the price before enrolling.

If your well-being has improved but you've also made decent lifestyle adjustments since being accepted for an insurance policy, you can seek to be assessed for a risk class change. Your rates will not increase even if it is discovered that your health is worse than it was at the time of underwriting. You should anticipate your premiums to drop if you're deemed to be in better health.

Let's break down the procedure into a few steps:

Step 1 – Figure Out How Much You Will Need

Consider what expenditures would need to be met if you were to pass away. Mortgages, college fees, and other loans, not to mention burial costs, are all examples. Furthermore, if your spouse or dear ones require an income stream and are unable to give it on their own, income replacement is critical. There are internet calculators that may help you calculate the lump payment that will cover any prospective charges.

Step 2 – Preparing Application

You need to figure out the things which are going to affect your life insurance cost and premiums. Factors that most often affect insurance policy are:

- **Age:** Life expectancy is the major of all determinants of risk for any insurance policy.
- **Gender:** Women tend to pay lower rates for the premiums since they have a longer life expectancy statistically.
- **Well-being:** Medical analysis is necessary for

the majority of the policies. Their tests involve screening for diabetes, heart disease, cancer, along with other medical conditions which may develop over time.

- **Smoking:** A smoker is at risk for a variety of health problems that can shorten life and raise risk-based premiums.
- **Medical History:** It could be a major drawback if you have any medical history of potential diseases. Your risk of developing or contracting certain conditions becomes much higher.
- **Driving Record:** Insurance prices might skyrocket if you have a history of traffic infractions or driving while inebriated.
- **Lifestyle:** Premiums might spike if you live a destructive lifestyle.

Family medical histories, as well as beneficiary information, are typically required on life insurance applications. You'll almost certainly have to undergo a medical examination and declare any pre-existing medical disorders, traffic tickets, or DUIs, as well as any risky pursuits like motorsport or paragliding.

Standard kinds of identification, such as your social security card, U.S. passport, or driver's license will be required prior to a policy being drafted.

Step 3 – Comparisons of Insurance Quotes

After you've gathered all of the data you'll need, you may get numerous quotations from various suppliers depending on your search. Prices might vary significantly from one business to the next; however, it's crucial to shop around for the greatest policy, business rating, and premium price. Since you'll be paying for life insurance on a periodic basis for years, finding the right coverage to meet your needs can save you a good amount of money.

Benefits of Life Insurance

There are certain advantages to owning insurance coverage. The most essential benefits and safeguards provided by life insurance plans are discussed here. The majority of individuals buy life insurance with the purpose of providing income to dependents who would be financially disadvantaged if the insured died. The tax benefits of life insurance, such as tax-deferred development of dollar value, tax-free death benefits, and tax-free dividends, can give extra strategic options for affluent individuals.

Dodging taxes, a life insurance policy's fatality reward is commonly free of tax. High earners may get perpetual life insurance through a trust to facilitate paying estate taxes when they pass away. This method aids in the preservation of the estate's worth for their successors. Tax avoidance differs from tax evasion, which is illegal, in that it is a law-abiding approach for reducing one's tax burden.

Before You Buy Insurance

Given that life insurance plans are such a large investment and commitment, it's vital to conduct thorough due diligence to ensure that the firm you pick has a proven track record and financial stability, especially considering your family may not get a death benefit for years.

Life insurance could be a wise financial instrument in hedging your chances and providing security for your family members if you pass away whilst the policy is active. Yet, there seem to be times when it seems illogical, such as when you buy far too much and insure people who do not really need their income replaced. As a result, it's critical to think about the following:

What obligations would you be unable to cover if you died? If your partner makes a good living and you do not even have any kids, this might not be necessary. It will still be crucial to think about the impact of your passing affecting your spouse, as well as how much financial help they would need to mourn without having to worry over going back to work until they're prepared.

When both partners' incomes are required to sustain a current lifestyle or satisfy financial obligations, each partner might require individual life insurance coverage.

If you're obtaining a life insurance policy for a member of the family, you should ask yourself, "What is it that I am attempting to insure?" Seniors and children do not have much money to replace, yet funeral costs may need to be met in the case of their passing. A parent may desire to safeguard their child's future term insurance by getting moderately sized insurance while they are young, in addition to burial costs. This permits the parent to ensure that their child's future family is financially secure.

Is it possible to make a higher return on the money spent on premiums for perpetual insurance during the length of a policy? If a substantial income isn't needed to be replaced or if policy investment returns on cash worth are unduly cautious, constant saving and investing—for instance, self-insuring—might make more sense in some situations as a buffer against unpredictability.

7

WRITING YOUR WILL

*A*lmost all of us are familiar with what a will is and why it is used. However, in this chapter, we will try to draw a picture of the salient points of a will and why you need one in your retirement. To have a rough idea, a will is thought to be some kind of legal document which is drawn up for the distribution of your property or assets.

Let's take a deeper look at what a will actually is and how it can help you. A will is a legal document that expresses your desires for the division of your assets and the protection of any underage children. Those desires might not even be followed if you die without a will. Furthermore, your beneficiaries may end up spending more time, wealth, and mental engagement settling your affairs after you're dead.

Wills differ in efficacy based on the kind, but still, no document is likely to negotiate each difficulty that emerges following your death. Unwillingness to make a will usually means that choices concerning your property are made by courts or state officials, which can lead to family turmoil.

Anyone can write a legitimate will on their own, but you must get the document witnessed to reduce the possibility of future potential challenges. Think about having your will created by a trust and estates attorney to ensure that everything is in order.

Why Is a Will Necessary?

Many people believe that wills are only necessary for the very rich or those with complex holdings. Nonetheless, there are other compelling reasons for having a strong will, which may include:

- Specifying who claims your assets. You have authority over who receives what part and how much.
- Protection of your property from certain estranged relatives (who may be eyeing your property too well).
- Deciding upon who will be the guardian of your children. Although courts can decide this if no one is mentioned.
- Allowing your heirs to have quicker access by simple means to your assets.
- Arranging to save money on taxes for your

heirs. You might as well make contributions to charity and gifts to offset the estate tax.

It's Best to Have a Witness

Prepare a testamentary will to increase the possibility that your preferences will be carried out. It is the most popular sort of will; you draft the document and afterward sign it in a witness's presence. It's undoubtedly the finest insurance against effective objections to your preferences by surviving family members or professional acquaintances. You may draft one personally, but for added security, get it written by an estate attorney you trust.

Other Kinds of Wills

Although a testamentary will is probably your best chance, various other forms of wills are recognized to varying degrees. By knowing them all, you can decide which one is the most suitable for you.

- **Holographic Wills**

Wills put in writing by the testator that have not been witnessed are referred to as holographic wills, which derive from the less frequent secondary definition of the word holograph. It refers to a document penned by its creator. These wills are frequently used when time is limited and eyewitnesses are unavailable, such as when the testator is caught in a life-threatening catastrophe.

Many nations, however, do not accept holographic wills. In places where the papers are legal, the will must fulfill bare minimums, such as evidence that the testator created it and had the mental ability to do so. In addition, the lack of witnesses frequently leads to objections to the will's legality.

- **Oral Wills**

These wills by name can be understood to involve speaking only. The testator gets vocal about his wishes and desires in front of the witnesses. Unfortunately, many courts do not accept such wills–lacking a written record.

- **Pour-Over Wills**

A pour-over will be used in combination with the creation of a trust inside which your property will be transferred.

- **Mutual Wills**

This kind of will is generally drawn up by married couples in pursuance of their combined wishes and desires. When one partner dies, the other is obligated to abide by the drawn-up will.

Mutual wills are generally considered to guarantee that the deceased's property belongs to the deceased's heirs instead of a new spouse. Due to state variances in contract law, a mutual will must be prepared with the assistance of a legal practitioner. A mutual will must not be mistaken with a joint will, despite the fact that the phrases seem similar.

Purpose of a Will

A will enables you to specify how your assets, such as real estate, bank accounts, or valued things, should be dispersed. If you own an enterprise or have investments, your will can stipulate who receives them and when.

You can also allocate assets to a charity (or charities) of your choice through a will. Likewise, if you want to transfer assets to a certain organization or group, a will helps ensure that your desires are followed.

Although wills normally protect the majority of your property, they do not cover all of it. Payouts from the testator's life insurance policy are among the omissions. The insurance's beneficiaries will get the funds since they were named in the plan. The same would likely be true for any investment accounts labeled as "transfer on passing."

There seems to be one important exception: If the recipients of those resources predeceased the testator, the plan or account reverts towards the property and is divided up per the contexts of a will or, neglecting that, by a superior court branch of the judicial system that deals with wills, estates, and related matters.

Most states have elective-share or community property laws that make it illegal to disinherit one's spouse. A court may overrule a will if it distributes a lesser amount of such assets to the surviving spouse than state law requires, which is often between 30% and 50% (Smith, 2021).

A will not only directs your possessions, but it also specifies who should be appointed as guardian of your young children in the case of your death.

What If I Don't Have a Will?

If you pass away without a will, the state controls the distribution of your assets, which it will normally allocate using a predetermined formula.

Due to the obvious above-mentioned elective-share and community property laws, the formula tends to result in half of your inheritance passing to your spouse and the other half passing to your kids. In such a case, the family house or other assets may be sold, which can have a detrimental impact on a surviving spouse who may have relied on the majority of your assets to sustain their level of life.

If your children are young, the court may appoint a representative to care for their concerns. Dying without a will may also have fiscal implications because a correctly designed will can lower estate tax liabilities. Individual estates valued at $11,700,000 or more must submit a U.S. estate tax return by 2021. If the estate is worth less than that amount, no federal estate tax is required (Smith, 2021).

Begin to Prepare Your Will

To begin preparing a will, make a list of your possessions and obligations. Include the items of family heirlooms, safe deposit boxes, and any other property you want to pass to a specific person or business.

If you want to give certain personal goods to certain heirs, make a list of those allocations to include in your will later. Furthermore, you can choose the receivers of certain items in a separate paper known as an instruction letter, which would be maintained with the will. Nonetheless, if you just put instructions inside this letter, be sure the document is legally enforceable in your state; certain states do not accept them.

The instruction letter might be drafted in a somewhat more casual manner than the will. It may also include information that may assist your executor in settling your property, such as account information, passwords, and even funeral directions. The others will addenda, such as a medical directive, a power of attorney, or a living will, which can govern how a person's affairs are handled if he or she proves to be physically or mentally incompetent.

If both you and your partner lack willpower, you may be compelled to create a single document that covers both of you. Fight the temptation. Joint wills are nearly universally discouraged by estate planners, and some states do not even recognize them. Independent wills make better sense, even though yours and your spouse's wills may wind up appearing uncannily identical. (As previously stated, a joint will is not the same as a mutual will.)

How to Write a Will and Have It Validated

A proper will may not always necessitate expert assistance. Many software tools, as well as other DIY websites, are able to help you if you are inclined to take care of the work on your own. After you've completed the paperwork, it must be attested by two individuals who are mentally competent and familiar with you.

A witness to your will can be anybody, but it's ideal to choose an unbiased witness—someone who has never been a beneficiary and has no personal or financial interest in your decisions. In certain states, two or even more witnesses are required. If the will was written by a lawyer, they will not be one of the witnesses.

A will must be validated in some places, so verify the requirements where you reside. Even though it's not needed, you might want to have your witnesses sign a self-proving affidavit. The document, which must be signed in the presence of a notary, may speed up the probate procedure by decreasing the number of witnesses who must appear in court to verify their signatures and the will's validity.

Choosing Your Will's Executor

The executor of the estate must be someone who is still alive. The property is administered by that individual, who is usually a spouse, older child, or perhaps another trustworthy relative or friend. Joint executors, such as your spouse or partner and your attorney, can also be nominated.

The executor is frequently overseen by the probate court to make sure that the will's wishes are carried out. If your interests are complex and difficult, you may want to appoint an attorney or somebody with financial and legal skills.

If your property is large (mostly in millions of dollars)

or your position is legally complicated, hiring a professional is a good idea. If that's the case, make sure you consult with somebody who is aware of the laws in your area and has a lot of experience making wills. Your state bar organization might well be able to assist you in finding an appropriate lawyer.

Empowering your executor to pay your payments and deal with debt collectors is one of the most critical things your will can accomplish. Make sure that the phrasing of your will provides for this and that your executor has the authority to deal with any concerns that aren't clearly addressed in your will.

Keeping the Will

Before a probate court can process your property, it normally wants access to your initial will. It's critical, however, to preserve the document securely while giving access to it. Avoid placing money in a bank safe deposit box or somewhere else where your relatives could require a court ruling to have access to it. A home safe that is both waterproof and fireproof is a smart choice.

Finally, at the very least, tell your executor where the genuine will is kept, as well as any other pertinent information, such as the safe's key. It's also a good idea to give signed copies to the executor and, if you have one, your attorney. If the original is lost, the signed duplicates might be used to prove your intentions. The loss of an original will, on the other hand, might make things more complicated, and there's no assurance that your estate will be resolved as you'd wanted. As a precaution, keep the document secure.

Changing a Will

You may never have to revise your will. You can also opt to refresh it regularly. Keep in mind that the only copy of your will that counts is the one that is current and valid at the time of your passing.

A reasonable rule of thumb is to update your will every two to three years, as well as during significant life events. Wedding, separation, or the birth of a child are examples of such occurrences. After they've reached adulthood, your children are unlikely to require guardians listed in a will.

It is simple to alter your will. You can either replace the existing will with a new one or add to it with a codicil, which is a type of modification. Since codicils are so important and can amend the whole will, and two witnesses are normally made to sign them, just as they were when the original will was written. Nevertheless, several jurisdictions have eased the legal restrictions on codicils, allowing them to be certified at a common registrar.

Preferably, you should make any adjustments while you're in excellent health and mentality. This reduces the risk of your wishes being successfully contested and prevents hasty or emotionally charged judgments.

Living Will

Living will is similar to the general will, however, this kind involves your medical wishes and preferences. A living will is a planning strategy that gives you authority over healthcare choices if you become seriously sick or reach the end of your life. It informs people whether you wish to employ life-prolonging therapies such as feeding tubes and breathing machines. A living will is frequently combined with a durable medical power of attorney to form an outline. Living will forms can be found in a variety of locations, including online and in medical centers.

Death is something that no one wants to think upon. It's uncomfortable, unpleasant, and occasionally terrifying. Over the last 50 years, there has been extensive legislation in the United States to honor a person's ultimate wishes, particularly for individuals who are unable to speak for themselves (Christian, 2021a).

According to 2016 research published in Health Affairs, only around 30% of persons in the United States have signed a living will. People with chronic diseases were just marginally more likely than healthy people to put down their end-of-life desires, according to the study (Christian, 2021a).

A living will serves as a travel guide with key principles, yet they cannot account for every eventuality. This is why it is crucial to communicate. Whether or not you create a living will, family members and caretakers should be informed of your wishes.

Generally, living wills are utilized in situations like:

- Stroke
- Coma

- Dementia (advanced)
- Extreme brain injury
- Persistent vegetative state
- Other end-stage conditions

An advance directive is created by combining a living will with medical power of attorney. Living wills are valuable to people of all ages. If individuals do not convey their care wishes, especially young people, they can be gravely injured in accidents and left in a vegetative condition for years. Experts urge that everyone choose a trusted person to make vital medical choices on their account at the very least.

Making a Living Will

It's never fascinating to think about dying, but it's vital when creating a living will. Throughout this process, you will pose to yourself numerous questions, but one that is particularly crucial to contemplate is: What makes life worthwhile to you? Your response may be influenced by your religious or moral convictions. It might be impacted by personal experience in the past.

You must decide whether or not you need specific therapies and under what conditions. Should you want to be put on a ventilator if you had a possibility of recovering? What if it kept you living but prevented you from communicating with other people? How long do you think you'd like it to last? Are there just a few circumstances in which you'd consider it?

feeding tubes and ventilators, for example, can help save lives by giving the body time to recuperate. These efforts, on the other hand, may accomplish little beyond prolonging death at the end of existence, raising even more problems regarding quality vs. quantity of living. A list of potential life-prolonging methods is provided here:

- Organ donation
- If your breathing or heartbeat stops, you may need resuscitation
- Pain, nausea, and other symptoms may be relieved
- Artificial respiration (ventilator)
- Dialysis
- Feeding tube

Your feelings about these therapies may alter over time. Based on your health, your perception may change. For instance, a healthy 30-year-old's end-of-life care may be vastly different from that of an 80-year-old with stage-four cancer. Most papers can be cancelled or altered at a later date, as long as you are still capable of signing legal documents and are not disabled.

8

PENSION

*L*ast but not least, pensions are a major part of
your retirement nest egg. Pensions are generally
the retirement fund offered by your employer to
make your retirement survival easier. When the employee
retires, they receive an annuity based on the conditions of
their pension. Pension funds are significantly less wide-
spread than they formerly were, despite labor unions and
government workers accounting for the great bulk of
pension holders.

Pension is payments made to retired workers of an
organization in the form of an annuity over a certain
length of time as compensation for their previous employment with that company.

Manufacturing was once a pillar of the American
economy, employing thousands of folks over time. Many
of these employees belonged to labor organizations and
were guaranteed pensions when they retired. Conversely,

technological advancements and lucrative free-trade agreements resulted in a dramatic reduction in employment. Yet, when workers leave and no new ones are hired to replace them, the pension funds on which they rely to survive in retirement begin to shrink.

Traditional pension plans are becoming scarcer in the private sector of the United States. Pensions have mostly been substituted with less expensive retirement benefits for companies, including the 401(k) retirement savings plan.

According to the Bureau of Labor Statistics, around 83% of public employees and approximately 15% of private employees in the United States are now covered by a defined-benefit plan (Kagan, 2021).

Understanding Pension Plans

A pension plan needs payments from both the employee and the company, and it may provide for extra contributions from the employee. Wages are deducted to cover employee contributions. In addition, the employer could match a part of the employee's annual contributions up to a certain percentage or monetary amount.

Pension plans are classified into two types: defined benefit and defined contribution plans.

The Defined-Benefit Plan

In a defined-benefit plan, the company promises that the employee will earn a monthly fixed payment after retirement as well as for the rest of his or her life, irrespective of the value of the underlying investment pool.

As a result, the employer is responsible for a specified flow of pension payments to the retiree, in a monetary amount set by a system based on wages and years of service. The firm is responsible for the balance of the payment if the assets in the pension plan account are insufficient to cover all of the rewards that are payable.

Employer-sponsored defined-benefit pension plans stretch back to the 1870s. In 1875, the American Express Company launched its first pension plan. They covered 38% of all private-sector workers at their peak in the 1980s (Kagan, 2021).

The Defined-Contribution Plan

A defined contribution plan requires the employer to make a particular commitment for each employee covered by the plan. It might have been matched by employee contributions. The employee's final payout is determined by the investment performance of the plan. When the total contributions are depleted, the company's responsibility is terminated. Although the word "pension plan" is often used to refer to the classic defined-benefit plan, the 401(k) plan is a sort of defined-contribution pension plan.

A corporation may sponsor a defined contribution plan for significantly less money, yet the long-term expenses are harder to predict. They further commit the corporation to make up for any deficiencies in the fund.

As a result, an increasing number of independent employers are shifting to a defined benefit plan. The most well-known defined-contribution plans are the 401(k) and its non-profit version, the 403(b).

Verities

Several businesses provide both kinds of programs. Contributors can even roll over 401(k) balances into defined-benefit plans. Another option is the pay-as-you-go pension plan. These may be entirely funded by the employee, who can choose between salary deductions and lump sum payments (which are normally not allowed on 401(k) plans). They are otherwise comparable to 401(k) plans, with the exception that they never give a business match.

A pay-as-you-go pension plan is not the same thing as a pay-as-you-go financing mechanism. Existing employees' contributions are utilized to pay current beneficiaries for the latter. Pay-as-you-go programs, such as social security, are indeed an example.

Why Is Saving a Pension Good?

Why bother with a pension? Vast numbers of people are not saving close to enough to provide them with the level of life they desire when they retire. You have three options if you fall into this group. You may:

- Start saving earlier
- Retire later
- Lower your assumption of what can be affordable in retirement for you

It is critical not to rely on the state pension to sustain you in retirement. When you've finally started saving for retirement, you must select how you will do it. Pensions provide several benefits that will accelerate the growth of your money. A pension is essentially a tax-advantaged long-term savings scheme. When you receive tax relief on your pension, part of the funding that goes to the government as tax is instead put into your pension.

Your contributions are invested if you save through a defined contribution pension system. This is done so that they can develop during your working life and provide you with an income when you retire. In most cases, you may access the money in your pension pot after you reach the age of 55.

Employers are now required to enroll their employees in a workplace pension scheme to help them save more for retirement. This is known as 'automatic enrolling.' In some situations, irrespective of whether you participate in your pension, your employer will participate in it.

In other circumstances, you will be required to contribute as well. Even if they need you to contribute as well, remaining out is equivalent to turning down a salary raise unless you cannot afford to contribute or your priority is dealing with unsustainable debt. It's good to contribute to a pension to have additional money to spend later in life.

Consider whether you can manage to save based on your present budget and how much you would be likely to save if your situation changes, such as a pay raise. Consider how much money you'll need in retirement to live the lifestyle you choose.

· · ·

Pension Plans and Vesting

Participation in a defined-benefit plan is normally mandatory after one year of work; however, vesting might be immediate or delayed for almost seven to ten years. If you leave a firm before retiring, you may lose most or all of your pension benefits.

Individual contributions to defined contribution plans are fully vested as early as they are paid in. However, if your employer matches your contributions or provides you with company stock as part of a compensation package, it may establish a timetable in which a specific amount is transferred to you each term till you are 'fully vested.'

Nevertheless, just because your retirement payments are completely vested does not imply you may start withdrawing.

Pension Plans and Taxes

Most employer-sponsored pension plans are qualified, which means they fulfill the standards of Internal Revenue Code 401(a) and the Employee Retirement Income Security Act of 1974 (ERISA). This provides them with tax advantages for both companies and employees (Kagan, 2021).

Employee contributions to the plan are made from their paychecks; that is, they are deducted from the employee's total salary. This significantly decreases the employee's taxable income as well as the amount owed to the IRS on Tax Day. Funds invested in a retirement account grow tax-deferred, which means no tax is required on the funds while being saved in the account.

These types of plans enable the employee to postpone paying taxes on retirement plan profits unless withdrawals commence. This tax classification enables the employee to reinvest dividend payments, capital gains, and interest income, all of which yield a significantly greater interest rate in the years leading up to retirement.

When the account holder retires and begins taking funds from a qualifying pension plan, federal income taxes are payable. Several states would also tax the income.

How Much Will I Get?

This is determined by whether your pension is a defined-benefit or defined-contribution. You will receive a predetermined income if you have a defined-benefit pension plan. This is determined by your final pensionable income (or your average income during your employment) and decades of pensionable employment.

You establish your pot of money if you've had a defined contribution pension program. This pot's worth might rise or fall. However, pension funds often grow over time, and you may be eligible for numerous tax breaks. Upon retirement, the amount of funding you receive will be determined by the size of your pension pot plus however you choose to withdraw funds from your pension during that time.

Would it be too late to start putting money down for a pension? Irrespective of age, saving for a pension is indeed a smart idea, especially if your company is ready to contribute as well. It's also a tax-effective method to save money, and you may be likely to access some or all of what you save as a tax-free sum.

But what if I end up dying before I receive my pension? Throughout most situations, your pension system will pay you benefits in the event of a loss. Your dependents may be given an income if you are a member of a defined benefit pension system. Your immediate family members may be paid a lump amount if you are enrolled in a defined contribution plan. The lump amount is typically equal to the value of your investment. They also might be able to use the funds to get income on a regular or as-needed basis. It's critical to verify with your pension provider to see if death benefits are payable.

How Do Defined-Contribution Pension Plans Work?

This is a sort of pension in which the money you receive when you retire is determined by how much capital you put in as well as how much money increases. The pension fund is built up through your contributions and the contributions of your employer (if available), as well as investment returns and tax breaks. It is useful to conceive of defined contribution pensions in two stages:

Stage 1 – When You Are Working

When you retire, the size of your pension pool will be determined by:

- How much you contribute to your pension pot
- What costs your pension provider deducted from your pot
- How successful your investments have been
- How long you intend to save

- How much, if anything, your company contributes

The money is often invested in shares and stocks, as well as many other investments, only to increase the fund's value over time until you retire. Typically, you may invest in a variety of funds. However, keep in mind that the value of your assets might fluctuate.

Stage 2 – When You Reach Retirement

You do not have to cease working to start drawing income from your pension account, although you would have to be at least 55 years old (57 from 2028). When you begin taking money, you can withdraw roughly a quarter (25%) of your pension account as a one-time tax-free lump payment. The remainder can be utilized to generate taxable revenue, or one or more taxable lump-sum payments.

Workplace Pension

If you have an employer pension, your company determines the number of contributions you make to the plan. Contributions are normally a proportion of your income; however, they can also be monetary. The employer may establish minimum contribution levels which you and they must pay. There are minimal contribution levels if your program is set up for automatic enrollment.

Personal Pension

If you organize your pension, you will then have complete control over how often and how much you contribute to it. Based on how consistent your income is, you might set up a daily donation, such as a regular payment. You might also choose to make one-time contributions when you have extra money.

Using Pension to Make a Living

You can receive your pension pool through one of the alternatives below, or a combination of them, starting at the age of 55 (increasing to 57 in 2028). Some or all of these solutions may be appropriate for you based on your age and personal circumstances. The following are your primary choices for utilizing your defined-contribution pension in retirement:

Retain your pension funds — withdraw them later

Use your pension account to purchase a secured income for the rest of your life or a certain period, often referred to as a lifelong or fixed-term annuity. Although the income is taxed, you can choose to receive up to 25% of your pot as a one-time tax-free lump amount at the outset (sometimes more with particular plans) (Money Helper, n.d.).

- Use your pension pool to create a flexible retirement income. This is referred to as pension drawdown. You can take the maximum amount you're authorized to take as a tax-free lump sum (usually up to 25% of the pot), then utilize the rest to generate recurring taxable income (Money Helper, n.d.).
- Take several lump-sum withdrawals. Typically, the first 25% of any lump sum withdrawal from

your fund is tax-free. The remainder will be taxed (Money Helper, n.d.).

- Take your pension money all at once. Normally, the first 25% is tax-free, and the remainder is taxed.
- Select any combination of the above, utilizing various areas of your pot or separate pots.
- Pension plans and pension funds

A pension fund is a defined-benefit plan that is made up of pooled contributions from companies, unions, or other organizations. Pension funds, which are controlled by professional fund managers on account of a firm and its workers, have significant sums of cash that are among the biggest investment firms in many countries. Their activities have the potential to control the stock markets in which they are involved.

Generally, pension funds are free from capital gains tax. Their investment portfolio income is either tax-deferred or tax-free. A pension fund gives a fixed, prede-termined payment to employees after retirement, allowing them to budget for their future liabilities. The employer gives the most and cannot reduce pension fund payments retrospectively.

Employee donations that are made voluntarily may also be accepted. Benefits stay steady in a shifting economic situation since they are not dependent on asset returns. Companies can pay more to a pension fund and subtract more from their taxes than they can with a defined-contribution plan.

The pension fund might assist in financing early retirement to promote certain company strategies. A pension plan, on the other hand, is more complicated and expensive to set up and operate than other types of retirement programs. Employees have no voice in investment choices. Furthermore, if the minimum contribution criterion is not met or if excessive contributions are made to the plan, an excise tax is levied.

An employee's compensation is determined by his or her final pay and duration of service with the organization. A pension fund does not offer loans or early withdrawals. In-service distributions are not permitted for participants under the age of 59 and a half. Early retirement usually results in a lower monthly payment.

LEAVE A REVIEW

Leave a 1-Click Review!

Click here to leave a quick review!

I would be incredibly thankful if you could take just 60 seconds to write a brief review on Amazon, even if it's just a few sentences!

CONCLUSION

If you have read this book in its entirety, I must say you have learned and gained the keys to early and settled retirement. The experience of retirement can both be exciting and terrifying, depending on the route you choose for it. If you are smart enough to make your retirement nest egg a comfortable one, savings and investments can be satisfying.

We believe retirement is a new world that begins after your employment days are over. It is certainly a period of enjoying your golden days, and it must be made as comforting as possible. Of course, if you are a person attached to hard work and keeping yourself preoccupied with any kind of activity, then you can continue working after retirement, as well.

Post-retirement, you have many options to invest your days and time in. You could pursue that hobby you always wanted to but didn't have time for. Or even go traveling the world as you always dreamed of. All that is certainly possible if you plan your retirement thoroughly. Planning for retirement is a challenging task, undoubtedly, but once you have your master plan laid out, you will feel very confident with yourself.

To start your retirement planning, you must consider many things, such as the time of your retirement, your current income, your lifestyle, your savings, your investment, and even the period you wish to work. By considering these factors, you will ultimately have a clear picture of the retirement you are seeking.

You will have to start budgeting and saving up each penny for your retirement funds. As an American, you have several opportunities to retire within America. The government fully facilitates and looks after their senior citizens with social security and policies like that.

Once decided, move on to the next step for deciding how and what to save or even invest. There are many options for an employed American to save up for retirement or invest funds to secure a future. Being employed means many opportunities to save up and invest for your retirement. Your employer can offer to contribute to a 401(k) savings account or Roth IRAs, too. Or even facilitate a pension account for you.

Estate investment could also be a fantastic option. Other than that, we recommend that you downsize and save money throughout your life. Now, I get it, downsizing may seem daunting and quite stressful at first. However, it brings many advantages to your financial position. When you downsize, you save a lot of money.

You get to have new experiences and a change of lifestyle.

A fresh start often proves to be quite beneficial for your health. However, it does depend upon some factors to decide whether moving is good for you or a bad choice. Sure, owning a property has its perks, but renting can save you from any obligations. Responsibilities such as paying taxes and maintenance of the property are not your liability when you rent a home for yourself.

One thing to keep in mind is to have control over your emotions when you're moving or downsizing. Emotions can trigger us with impulsive attitudes. One might get caught in the guilt trip and end up shopping more than the budgeted amount just because they think it is a tough time in their life and it is okay to spend a little extra.

Other than downsizing, you must thoroughly research the medical securities for your retirement. Various policies cover your medical expenses in retirement; however, Medicare stands to be the most prominent one. You may have certain needs for your particular medical conditions. Perhaps you inherited some kind of medical history for diseases like diabetes or heart disease or even cancer.

If it just runs in your family, then you cannot avoid it. Then you will need medical insurance and safety when you reach old age and look for support. Therefore, you must decide which policies and which insurances are best for you, along with their cost and taxes. Budgeting plays a huge role in every aspect of retirement.

Especially if you have just decided to retire earlier than the predetermined time, you must prepare yourself for out-of-the-way sacrifices and giving up certain things. For instance, you can no longer go on weekend excursions every single week. Saving up those bucks over a few drinks is more important than waking up hungover the next day.

Then comes the writing of the will part. A will is something that is going to help loved ones when you pass away. It is going to help distribute your property and assets among your loved ones as per your directions. We say writing a will should be an important priority for you.

There are many kinds of wills but the most authentic one is the kind that is signed and witnessed by a trustee. Having a will that has witnesses and proper signatures stands authoritative when challenged in court. That is, it cannot be denied or neglected if someone ever tries to take advantage of your death and claim the assets which rightfully belong to your loved ones.

Write a will and declare who gets to have what. Nominate your beneficiaries and divide your assets as per your desire. If you prefer not to do so, the court shall do what must be done and distribute your property as it finds just. To avoid that, you should write your will and secure your property before someone tries to snap at your family after you pass away.

Lastly, go through precisely with the pension part. There are usually two kinds of options in pension. The defined-benefit plan and the defined-contribution plan. Both of these offer pensions; however, one is planned and fixed while the other depends on the investment performance. Pensions are a great way to ensure that your family is provided for even after your demise.

Retirement is a reward that requires a person to work throughout his life in order to enjoy the fruits in the end after his work is done. To have a wonderful retirement like the one you've always dreamed about, you must sometimes make substantial sacrifices in your career, but they are small in comparison to what you will receive in the end. We all wish you the absolute best of luck with your financial planning, and we hope you end up securing a comfortable and exciting retirement.

GIFT

Just For You!

A FREE GIFT TO OUR READERS

Tips for managing your personal finance that you can download and begin to implement right away! Scan QR code or visit link below:

http://oainc.activehosted.com/f/1

REFERENCES

Anspach, D. (2021, May 21). *Plan for Rising Health Care Costs in Your Retirement.* The Balance. https://www.thebalance.com/how-to-plan-for-health-care-costs-in-retirement-2388478

Christian, R. (2021a, January 13). *Living Wills: What You Need to Know.* Annuity.org. https://www.annuity.org/retirement/planning/living-will/

Christian, R. (2021b, July 7). *A Seniors Guide to Downsizing For Retirement.* RetireGuide. https://www.retireguide.com/guides/downsizing-for-retirement/#content

Daughtery, G. (2021, September 16). *Avoid the Downsides of Downsizing in Retirement.* Investopedia. https://www.investopedia.com/articles/personal-finance/061914/downsides-downsizing-retirement.asp

Daugherty, G. (2021, September 29). *Managing Your Money After You Retire.* Investopedia. https://www.investopedia.com/articles/retirement/05/managingincome.asp

DeMatteo, M. (2020, September 21). *Most Americans are behind on their retirement savings—here are some tips to catch up.* CNBC. https://www.cnbc.com/select/how-to-increase-savings/

Fidelity. (2021a, April 28). *Medicare questions | Eligibility, choices, and costs | Fidelity.* Www.fidelity.com. https://www.fidelity.com/viewpoints/retirement/understanding-medicare-options

Fidelity. (2021b, June 5). *5 ways HSAs can fortify your retirement | Fidelity.* Www.fidelity.com. https://www.fidelity.com/viewpoints/wealth-management/hsas-and-your-retirement

Folger, J. (2021, February 7). *Retirement: U.S. vs. Abroad.* Investopedia. https://www.investopedia.com/articles/personal-finance/100214/retirement-us-vs-abroad.asp

Greene, M. (2021, November 6). *Insurance.* Encyclopedia Britannica. https://www.britannica.com/topic/insurance

Kagan, J. (2021, August 30). *Pension Plan Definition.* Investopedia. https://www.investopedia.com/terms/p/pensionplan.asp

Lake, R. (2021a, July 26). *Here Are the Best Places to Retire Abroad.* Investopedia. https://www.investopedia.com/retirement/best-countries-to-retire/

Lake, R. (2021b, October 27). *How to Plan for Medical Expenses in Retirement.* Investopedia. https://www.investopedia.com/retirement/how-plan-medical-expenses-retirement/

Money Helper. (n.d.). *Defined Contribution Pension schemes.* MaPS. https://www.moneyhelper.org.uk/en/pensions-and-retirement/pensions-basics/defined-contribu-tion-pension-schemes

Parker, T. (2021, July 30). *Life Insurance After Retirement: Do You Need It?* Investopedia. https://www.investopedia.-com/articles/personal-finance/010716/do-you-need-life-insurance-after-you-retire.asp

Perman, C. (2011, March 30). *Gen Y and Retirement: Are Young People Saving?* Www.cnbc.com. https://www.cnbc.-com/id/42321520

Pinkasovitch, A. (2020, September 29). *5 key retirement-planning steps everyone should take.* Investopedia. https://www.investopedia.com/articles/retirement/11/5-steps-to-retirement-plan.asp

Probasco, J. (2021, April 8). *Should Retirees Own or Rent Their Homes?* Investopedia. https://www.investopedia.-com/articles/retirement/07/buy-rent.asp

Silvestrini, E. (2021a, May 3). *Retirement Lifestyle: How to Retire.* Annuity.org. https://www.annuity.org/retirement/lifestyle/

Silvestrini, E. (2021b, July 12). *Health Care Costs in Retirement: What to Expect, How to Plan.* Annuity.org. https://www.annuity.org/retirement/health-care-costs/

Silvestrini, E. (2021c, November 1). *Retirement Planning: Safety and Comfort in Your Golden Years.* Annuity.org. https://www.annuity.org/retirement/planning/

Smith, L. (2021, April 25). *What Is a Will and Why Do I Need One Now?* Investopedia. https://www.investopedia.-com/articles/pf/08/what-is-a-will.asp#why-you-should-have-a-will

Weliver, D. (2021a, October 15). How To Invest Money:

The Smart Way To Grow Your Money. *Money under 30.* https://www.moneyunder30.com/how-to-invest

Weliver, D. (2021b, October 15). *Retirement Guide for Late Starters: 14 Tips from Financial Experts.* Annuity.org. https://www.annuity.org/retirement/planning/retirement-guide-for-late-starters/

Which? Money Team. (2021, November 3). *Why should you downsize? - Which?* Which? Money. https://www.which.co.uk/money/pensions-and-retire-ment/financing-later-life-care/later-life-housing-options/should-you-downsize-aqcvn4w6kz0f